The Inside Scoop on God

By Deborah Erdmann

Table of Contents

God. Don't go camping without Him!

There's plenty of God to go around.

Click your heels to find your way back home.

Don't get caught with your pants down.

A mad race to claim favoritism from God.

The right reasons for holding off on that Snickers bar.

Do you ever feel trapped in your cage?

Are you using all of your body parts in your worship to God?

An alarm-ing look at how we try to hear God over all the noise.

Exchange your kingdom for God's.

A sweet story of the Father's love.

Who's helping who in your marriage?

It's okay to walk away when the world rejects you.

We've been using the wrong side of our brains to get to know God.

Greed and gluttony in hording God's manna.

If your life ended abruptly, would you be ready to meet your Maker?

All this talk about Adam, what about Eve and what she had to suffer?

Enjoying the day at hand.

Are we stressing or blessing with our prayers?

The shocking realization that God lives with us.

Preface

"Teach me your ways so I may know you." (Ex 33:13)

For years my relationship with God involved gracing the doorstep to many a church and religiously tuning in to God TV … but it still felt like something was missing. I knew *of* God, but I didn't sense that I really knew Him.

I know my husband. I don't just know *of* him, I *know* him. That's because we spend tons of time together. We have long talks, and we do nice things for each other. We laugh a lot too. It's a real relationship. One day it occurred to me—can I know God like that? The only thing I knew about Him was what I heard from preachers and teachers and televangelists. I decided to get up close and personal with God, with Jesus as my only mediator.

When I started spending daily quiet times with God, I began sensing His presence. I became aware that He was speaking to me through the Bible, One-on-one conversations, and sometimes in my dreams. I even began to feel His emotions and feelings about common everyday situations. In the midst of these interactions, I began to sense His care for me was more than I ever realized, and I found myself falling in love with Him. Now, as with my husband, I don't want to live without Him.

I was chasing Him, and occasionally He would let me pin Him down. You are holding in your hands the chain reaction to my sanguine pursuit of God. And to think it all happened in my living room. I guess you could say I'm a couch potato for Christ.

It's all about knowing God … one scoop at a time.

1

FAMILY CAMPOUT

"Behold, I stand at the door and knock; if anyone hears
My voice and opens the door, I will come in to him and
will dine with him, and he with Me." (Rev 3:20)

"We now no longer camp as for a night but have settled
down on earth and forgotten heaven."
(Henry David Thoreau)

Let's go on a camping adventure! Do you like to camp? Cool nights under the stars, roasting marshmallows over a crackling fire. Picking said marshmallows out of your hiking boots after you've walked a mile in the dirt. Stumbling over some poor sap curled up in his sleeping bag in your clumsy attempt to find the bathroom in the middle of the night. Good times.

In the book of Exodus, the Israelites went on the biggest camping caravan ever. They traveled across the desert, towing lock, stock and barrel along with them. This was one big family outing. Can't you just picture everyone sitting around the campfire, laughing and telling stories?

I imagine God liked to look down on them from His abode above and smile. Maybe He wished He could camp with them, but the problem was, they didn't know Him very well. So, He invited them to come and visit Him around His smoking mountain. "He's like— "Come, gather around! I have a nice big campfire going for you." Moses even gave them the handwritten invitations. What was their response? "Speak to us yourself and we will listen. But do not have God speak to us, or we will die" (Ex 20:19).

So then God said, "Then have them make a sanctuary for me, and I will dwell among them" (Ex 25:8). And He made a huge list of the things He would like inside it. So basically, what He said was, "Since you won't come to Me, I'll come to you. I want to camp with you! I'll decorate my tent with gold and silver and bronze, fine linens and cherubim and such. It will be really cool!" The Maker of the universe desired to be with His people so much that He was willing to pitch tent when He could have lived on a cloud.

But guess where God ended up camping? "Now Moses used to take the tent and pitch it outside the camp some distance away …" (Ex 33:7). They're like "Uh, okay. He can hang around, but not too close." They treated Him like a homeless drifter, or like one of those relatives they'd rather not admit being related to. (We all have one of those. If you don't know who yours is—it's probably you!) Their clannish separation kept God out of their campground.

So, God finally takes a hint, and tells them, "Go up to the land flowing with milk and honey. But I will not go with you, because you are a stiff-necked people and I might destroy you on the way" (Exodus 33:3). Maybe Moses could have negotiated a deal. Say, instead of killing them, a week without manna and a severe beating. Who could blame Him? They all wanted the promised land, but not the One who made the promises.

God tried again to be a presence among His people when He had King Solomon build a house for Him in Jerusalem with all of the silver and gold and kingly treasures. God promised He would hear the prayers of His people in this place, as long as they would keep His laws and walk in His ways. Solomon answered, "But will God really dwell on earth with humans? The heavens, even the highest heavens, cannot contain you. How much less this temple I have built!" (2 Chron 6:18). Indeed! Sadly, they did not walk in His ways, thus God eventually abandoned the house.

Finally, God sent His spoken Word to live as a Son and bring to light His desire to camp among His kids. This time He delivered His invitation through Jesus Christ. God actually shed His own blood through Jesus on Calvary to show His love for us. Will we now invite Him to our campfire? IF I HAVE ANYTHING TO SAY ABOUT IT WE WILL! Heheh.

So, let's do this campout the right way, with the Lord of the star-studded sky and smoky mountain sitting right beside us. Each day as you're settling in to read one of these stories, invite God to sit around the campfire with you. You can light a candle and stick a marshmallow over it if you like. And you don't even need Moses to mediate between you and God. It'll be just you … and God. Enjoy the adventure! Pass the marshmallows …

2

HOARDING GOD

"And do not forget to do good and to share with others,
for with such sacrifices God is pleased." (Heb 13:16)

"We are not cisterns made for hoarding, we are
channels made for sharing."
(Billy Graham)

With all the busyness in this fast-paced world, it can become increasingly difficult to get alone with God. And when you're raising a family, a few minutes of time alone with God can be slim to none. If you're like me you like to worship God with your eyes closed and tune out the rest of the world so you can give God your full attention. Not an easy thing to do when you're seldom alone.

A few years ago, my alone time with God consisted of going up to my bedroom, locking myself in and completely ignoring my beloved children's relentless banging on the door to get my attention (they were teenagers at the time, so no need to call Social Services). "Mom—I'm starving, and there's nothing here to eat. Mom, it's my turn for the computer and they won't get off. Mom …" well, you get the picture.

Of course, I would lay down the law beforehand— "No one is to bother me under any circumstances. I need my God-time, so I don't kill all of you!" But none of that did any good. I would be in the middle of my prayers, when I would have to stop to feed the poor hungry children or break up World War III. Oddly, when I would finally get back upstairs to God, I could no longer feel His presence. So, I would yell to my kids "Now look what you did—you scared God away!"

I think the reason I need to have God all to myself

stems from growing up in a large family. At times it was a real battle to have anything for myself. There were always other people to consider and to share with. Sometimes at the dinner table we had to draw our weapons in order to get enough food to eat.

I remember on one occasion my parents bought a gallon of ice cream, a rare treat at our house. We lined up for our ice cream cones, and then I wittingly watched as my brothers and sisters furiously licked their cones like they were in an "all you can eat" competition, while I, with colossal determination (the likes of which higher powers possess) licked mine slowly in order to be the only remaining ice cream cone contender. But the fates were cruel. They all ran back to the kitchen and received seconds, so I quickly downed mine and ran to the kitchen for more, only to find out the ice cream was all gone.

I'm in good company wanting time alone with God. According to Luke 5:16, Jesus wanted the same thing. He often withdrew to lonely places to pray, to get His daily God fix. But He didn't get filled up with God just to keep it to Himself. He went back to the crowds empowered with the Holy Spirit so that He could share the gospel, heal the sick and set the captives free.

Hebrews 13:16 exhorts us to share with others. Have we been sharing God? I wonder what kind of world this would be if we all got our daily dose of God and kept it to ourselves. Have you ever seen a hoarder's house? They can't bring themselves to get rid of anything, so the clutter keeps piling up … newspapers, knick-knacks, even garbage.

What would our hearts look like if we were hoarding the things of God? If we would keep asking to be filled with the Holy Spirit every day and then keep it all to ourselves, we would self-destruct. God's love isn't meant to be contained. It's poured into us so we can pour it into others. And the more we pour out, the more that gets poured back into us to pour right back out. It's kind of like a laundry cycle. Wash, rinse, dry, repeat.

One day as I was driving alone in my car, my thoughts drifted off to something a famous evangelist once said. He dreamt that he was in heaven, and there were thousands of people lined up before the throne, waiting to see God. The thought of having to wait for any amount of time to see God alarms me. So, I said to Him, "God? When I get to heaven will I ever be able to be alone with You?" Just then I sensed God was saying, "You're alone with me right now, but please don't talk to Me with your eyes closed when you're driving!"

Have you been in that lonely place with God? The place where you desperately seek more of God's presence? That's cool, but don't keep it all to yourself. Save some of that for me.

3

THERE'S NO PLACE LIKE HOME

"God left him to test him and to know everything that was in his heart." (2 Chron 32:31)

"Close your eyes and tap your heels together three times. And think to yourself, there's no place like home." (The Wizard of Oz)

My son Aaron has been scarred for life—at least that's his take on the terrible tragedy that befell him when he was four years old. We went to KFC for dinner, and then afterwards we all piled into our station wagon and headed for home. Halfway home one of the kids in the back of the car yelled, "Where's Aaron?" Where indeed! We must have forgotten him at KFC!

Mark hit the brakes, did a 180, and drove at breakneck speed back to the restaurant. A car drove past us on the way and the driver stuck his head out of the window and yelled, "Hey! You forgot your kid at KFC!" "We know!" we yelled back and sped even faster.

When we pulled into the parking lot we saw Aaron standing forlornly in the window, tears streaming down his cheeks. An employee came over and explained that he had offered Aaron some pudding after we abandoned him, but Aaron didn't want any pudding.

How must my sweet baby boy have felt when his family deserted him? He probably wondered if we were ever coming back. And how must he have felt when a man in a paper hat walks up to him and says, "Tough break kid! Here, have some pudding."

I went through my own abandonment crisis not too long ago. I was at a Christian conference in Las Vegas, having the time of my life, when God decided to check out of the party early. All of a sudden, I couldn't feel His presence with me. Now I know what it would feel like on this earth without God's presence—sheer hell!

I suddenly felt as though I were an alien on this strange, God-forsaken planet. Even though it was 110 degrees in Las Vegas, I made Mark take me to Target to buy pants and a long-sleeved shirt so I wouldn't feel so vulnerable.

For two days I approached every pastor and speaker at that conference, pleading with them to bring God back to me, but nothing took. As a last resort I asked the church receptionist to help me. (I was going through a phase where I thought only pastors could hear from God.) I explained to her that I was lost, and I didn't know how to get back home.

"Where is home?" she asked.

"Home is wherever God's presence is," I said.

She sat quietly in thought for a while, and then suddenly she cried, "You're in the fire! God is testing you to see what you'll do when you can't find Him. He's been waiting; all you have to do is make the first move." That was it? The whole time I was waiting for God to make a move, He was waiting for me? And here I was, playing Marco Polo all by myself.

Immediately I felt the Holy Spirit bubbling up inside me. God was back! Not only did I know it, she knew it. She said, "When you came in here, your eyes looked dead. I was really worried about you. But now your eyes are shining like diamonds."

On the airplane heading home the next day, I was paging through a magazine when I came across a picture of Dorothy from the Wizard of Oz, wearing those classic red heels. I couldn't help but chuckle to myself. The whole time I had been lost, it was just a matter of clicking my heels to find my way back home.

Though I can't say for sure what that disappearing act was all about, I suspect God was teaching me a lesson. In the future, whenever God starts feeling far away, I can't just sit and wait for Him to make the first move. I have to make it. "Marco …?"

God has promised that he will never leave nor forsake us, but he never promised that we will always feel His presence. David was a man after God's own heart, yet even he cried, "Why, Lord do you reject me and hide your face from me?" (Psalm 88:14). Job had a similar time of distress, in which God seemed to be M.I.A. (Job 23:8-10).

I have come to learn that this is a normal part of the testing and maturing of our faith. This is "the winter of the heart." It is sheer terror to experience this separation, but it's vital for the development of our faith. Sometimes it takes picturing life *without* God before we can start appreciating life *with* Him.

Are you feeling lost? Repeat after me: "There's no place like home. There's no place like home. There's no place like home." Still here? Tough break, kid. Have some pudding.

4

PANTS ON THE GROUND

"Therefore keep watch, because you do not know the day or the hour." (Matt 25:13)

"I am prepared to meet my Maker. Whether my Maker is prepared for the great ordeal of meeting me is another matter." (Winston Churchill)

Something really funny happened the other day. Our neighbor Clara called, crying "Help! I've fallen and I can't get up!" (That wasn't the funny part.) When we got there, we found her lying on the floor in her pajamas next to the bed with a pile of old pictures and books beside her. We asked where all that junk came from and she explained that as long as she was just lying there, she would make herself useful and clean the mess under her bed. I thought that was hilarious!

I was impressed by that, but not surprised. You see, Clara is no slacker. She grew up on a farm, so hard work is no stranger to her. Even when she's stranded on the floor, she makes herself useful.

If that were me on the floor, I'd probably just lie there and daydream of chocolate-covered potato chips and tropical beaches. I wouldn't feel all that guilty if I couldn't clean my house right then and there. The only chore that could get me off the floor is a shopping trip, because I don't really need sanitation, but I can always use a good pair of pants.

Speaking of pants, remember this episode from Seinfeld?

Kramer: I was returning some pants. I took a short cut in a subway tunnel and fell in some mud, ruining my pants. The very pants I was returning.

Elaine: I don't understand. You were wearing the pants you were returning?

Kramer: Well, I guess I was.

Elaine: What were you going to wear home?

Kramer: Elaine, are you listening? I never made it to the store.

Funny stuff, and a perfect visual of the mess we get ourselves into when we don't plan ahead. Matthew 25:13 is a warning to stay on our toes, to be prepared. When Jesus comes back in the clouds, we're going to miss that grand and glorious entrance if we're not prepared to take our place alongside Him, and we sure don't want to get caught with our pants down. You know what *that* means— "Pants on the ground. Pants on the ground. Looking like a fool with your pants on the ground."

How can we make sure we're ready? We can learn a lesson from the five virgins who didn't have any oil in their lamps when they went to meet the Bridegroom (Matt 25:1-13). The Holy Spirit is the oil, and we need to be filled daily.

I start my day with God. "In the morning, LORD, you hear my voice; in the morning I lay my requests before you and wait expectantly" (Psalm 5:3). Then I take God with me the rest of the day. Waiting expectantly means I'm anticipating His every move. He doesn't just want part of our day—He wants all of it.

God's continual Presence is a promise, equipping us for every situation. Yet we often go through the day unaware of Him. How that must grieve Him! Once we learn to walk in His Presence 24/7, then we never have to worry about missing the boat—we'll be in it.

And lastly but not leastly, you should always keep a Bible handy, in case you ever fall down and can't get up. Make yourself useful while you're lying on the floor doing nothing.

Got God?

5

I'M GOD'S FAVORITE!

"The disciple whom Jesus loved was reclining next to him." (John 13:23)

"I know we're all God's children, but sometimes I think He likes me extra special." (Doug, King of Queens)

18

I'm really starting to get annoyed with the Book of John. The gospels of Matthew, Mark and Luke weren't written in this arrogant manner; none of those disciples refer to themselves as "the disciple Jesus loved." In John's gospel, this statement is made so many times, I'm developing quite an attitude about this guy. I can understand someone introducing themselves as "the disciple who loved Jesus," but not the other way around.

I like to daydream that I'm walking around in heaven enjoying the divine opportunity for "meet and greets;" shaking the hands of all the great men and women of renown; the prophets and priests whose stories have been recorded in the best-selling book of all time. But all of a sudden in the middle of my daydream, John comes walking up to me and offers his hand—I don't know if he wants me to shake it or kiss it—and he says, "Hello! I'm the disciple Jesus loves!"

Did Jesus have favorites? Among his exclusive group of twelve disciples, only three (John, James and Peter) were invited to accompany Jesus to behold his glory on the mount of transfiguration (Matt 17:1), and to share his sorrow in the garden of Gethsemane (Matt 26:37). And to narrow it down even further, only one of those three (John) leaned on Jesus' chest (John 13:25). What a display of love and intimacy!
Why was John the only one who got to do that? Why didn't anyone else get to lean on Jesus' chest? And the

thought came to me like a light bulb moment—maybe John was the only one who wanted to!

I suppose this kind of intimacy doesn't come across as manly to a lot of guys. The other disciples might have just shook Jesus' hand when they felt a sudden surge of emotions, or tossed him a candy bar to shower Him with affection. Heck, they probably didn't even know it was possible to stake the claim for favoritism. All they knew was that they were getting annoyed with John's incessant bragging. *Just what does a guy have to do in order to become Jesus' favorite?* Therein lies the answer. I believe that the minute you pose that question to Jesus, He answers … "Yer in!"

Back in the day (BC), I used to haunt a club in Milwaukee called The Safe House. The Safe House is a refuge for spies engaging in covert operations. Fine … it's a pub, okay? (I did say "BC," so no rock-throwing is called for). In order to get in, you had to know the password. Learning the password usually involved sitting on the curb and waiting for the drunken sailors to come out and enlighten you. If you didn't know the classified, top-secret password, you couldn't get in.

So, pretend I'm the drunken sailor with your life-saving password. Here it is: "Ask and you shall receive." It doesn't get any easier than that. Do you want to lean on Jesus' chest, or call yourself His favorite? Go ahead! We're all the "disciples who Jesus loves." It's ours for the asking. Name it and claim it. Blab it and grab it. You and I are totally copacetic, home fry.

Someday when I finally get to heaven, I'm going to walk around introducing myself with my own special greeting. "Hello! I'm the disciple Jesus loves!" And if I happen to bump into John, well, I guess we'll just have to arm wrestle for that title.

6

TO FAST OR NOT TO FAST

"After 40 days and 40 nights of going without eating,
Jesus was hungry."
(Matt 4:2 NIRV)

"There are people in the world so hungry, that God
cannot appear to them except in the form of bread."
(Charles Dickens)

Just thinking about going on a fast makes me hungry. It's like my brain starts sending signals to my stomach: "All hands and forks on deck—the captain is walking the plank!" So, my stomach responds by setting anchor at the next port and stocking up on potato chips and Snickers bars.

The longest fast I ever attempted was a liquid-only fast for seven days. I made it to the fifth day, but then my family had the audacity to order pizza. I caved. It was pizza, okay? Pizza! The pizza won. The next morning my growling stomach woke me up, looking for more pizza. I figured since I already broke my fast the night before, I might as well eat.

Apparently, God had different plans. As I lie there with visions of French toast sticks dancing in my head, I suddenly had a sick feeling in the pit of my stomach. I rolled over towards Mark, and groaned, "Oh, no!"

"What's wrong now?" Mark retorted. (Note to self: don't start whining before Mark has his coffee.)

"I don't think God will let me eat breakfast!"

"Just go ahead and eat," he said. "Problem solved. Now go back to sleep."

I immediately headed downstairs, confident that I could eat, since Mark said it was okay. (And in case

God should question me, I would answer, "It was the man you gave me. He told me to eat.") I put some French toast sticks on a pan and put them in the oven. As I was waiting for the timer to go off, I started to sense God tapping me on the shoulder, asking, "What do you think you're doing?"

I tried reasoning with Him, explaining that I already broke my fast with last night's pizza so I might as well keep eating. He didn't budge. Then I reminded Him that wasting food is a sin. Still nothing. Finally, I gave in. "Fine," I said, "but don't come along later with a big guilt trip about all the hungry kids in China when I throw my French toast sticks in the garbage!"

I made it the rest of the week without too much complaining. On the seventh night, our son was healed at a prayer service. I finally understood why God wanted me to fast the entire week; it was for a miracle. I was so impressed by the logistics of it, that I started fasting one day a week from then on. I didn't fast for anything in particular, mostly for other people's prayer requests. I really thought I had struck gold with this new discovery, and I was determined to stick with this fasting regiment for the rest of my life. Plus, losing a few inches around my waist was the icing on the cake … though in this case, there was no cake in the deal.

But then I discovered God's take on this. Isaiah 58:5-7 paints a different picture of what God thinks of fasting. He said, "Is this the kind of fast I have chosen, only a day for people to humble themselves? Is it only for bowing one's head like a reed and for lying in sackcloth and ashes? Is that what you call a fast, a day acceptable to the LORD? Is not this the kind of fasting I have chosen: to loose the chains of injustice and untie the cords of the yoke, to set the oppressed free and break every yoke? Is it not to share your food with the hungry and to provide the poor wanderer with shelter—when you see the naked, to clothe them, and not to turn away from your own flesh and blood?"

And in Matthew 9:14-15 when John's disciples asked Jesus why His disciples didn't fast, he said, "How can the guests of the bridegroom mourn while he is with them? The time will come when the bridegroom will be taken from them; then they will fast."

So, I concluded that feeding the hungry was more important to God than just sitting at home with my stomach growling. And if Jesus said we should fast out of longing for the bridegroom, then I decided I would fast out of my longing for His presence, and not just because I want some physical answer to prayer. But then another question arose—how often and how long should I fast?

And then one day God answered my questions. Oh, this is good, are you ready? He said, "*There is no formula*.” Aha! God didn't want me to make a ceremony or ritual out of fasting; instead, it should be a matter of the heart, not a matter of rules and regulations. In a matter of seconds, I was in the kitchen pigging out on peanut butter.

7

I'M GROWING A GARDEN. CAN YOU DIG IT?

"You are God's field ..." (1 Cor 3:9)

"Judge each day not by the harvest you reap but by the
seeds you plant."
(Robert Louis Stevenson)

One day as I was surfing Christian television, a televangelist showed up on my TV screen asking for faithful partners to sow seeds into his ministry. If you've been on the Christian hamster wheel for any length of time, then you know this man wasn't asking for vegetable seeds to plant in his garden—he was asking for cold hard cash. He promised that this seed offering would result in a great harvest for me. Woo hoo!

I immediately reached for my checkbook to contribute my share toward this cash harvest. I sent my check off in the mail, and then sat back rubbing my hands together with glee, waiting for my ship to come in. It never did. Geez, did I just waste a perfectly good piece of paper?

Even if we had received a sudden surge of miracles, I still questioned my motives for this type of giving. Was I giving just to get something in return? I found myself searching for opportunities to give, to stock-pile rewards. "Let's see, how much should I give in order to get that foot massage spa I've been wanting?" (Sure, I have plenty of knick knacks. It's the lack of paddy whacks that concerns me.)

Then one day I stumbled upon Matthew 9:13: "I desire mercy, not sacrifice." When I applied this scripture to the area of giving, the light bulb guy in my head started doing cartwheels. God wanted me to give mercifully, not sacrificially!

Sowing seeds for profit doesn't seem merciful to me. "If you lend to those from whom you expect repayment, what credit is that to you? Even sinners lend to sinners, expecting to be repaid in full. But love your enemies, do good to them and lend to them *without expecting to get anything back* (Luke 6:34-36, italics added). Anytime we give to get, we miss the mercy boat.

Doing something out of duty or obligation doesn't seem merciful either. Maybe that's why God says He doesn't want sacrifices. He doesn't need our food or money (Ps 50:12). He owns the whole world. We're like, "Hey God, you can have my half-eaten Snickers bar and this crumpled dollar bill!" Send your chocolates and extra cash *my* way if you want to help someone needy, but God has no use for it. All He wants is for us to lend a helping hand to each other, and in that way, we're helping Him.

"I was hungry and you gave me nothing to eat, I was thirsty and you gave me nothing to drink, I was a stranger and you did not invite me in, I needed clothes and you did not clothe me, I was sick and in prison and you did not look after me.' "They also will answer, 'Lord, when did we see you hungry or thirsty or a stranger or needing clothes or sick or in prison, and did not help you?' "He will reply, 'Truly I tell you, whatever you did not do for one of the least of these, you did not do for me' (Matt 25:42-45).

Some kids down the road had a lemonade stand. I walked over and bought a cup of lemonade, and I couldn't help but smile at how excited this made them. That was so much fun, that I emptied my pockets and gave it to them as a tip.

These kids are learning that when life hands you lemons … you make lemonade. Mercy or sacrifice? Mercy.

We sat in church, and when the offering basket passed by, we placed our envelope in it. We didn't give this cheerfully; we gave out of duty. We didn't even know what the offering was for. God loves the cheerful giver for a good reason—it's supposed to feel good helping people. "Each of you should give what you have decided in your heart to give, not reluctantly or under compulsion, for God loves a cheerful giver" (2 Cor 9:7). Mercy or sacrifice? Sacrifice.

Cain and Abel both gave the Lord offerings (Gen 4:4-5). Cain gave fruits from the soil, and Abel gave the firstborn of his flock. God rejected Cain's offering. Doesn't God know that fruits and vegetables are good for you? No, it wasn't that He preferred animal offerings over fruit. My NIV study notes on Hebrews 11:4 say this: "It is implied that Cain's sacrifice was rejected because he offered it without faith, as *a mere formality*." Heaven help us if we do anything for God out of mere formality.

So I stopped planting seeds in a make-believe garden. I want something real, something I can get up to my elbows in. Right now, this contrary Mary is up to my elbows in weeds, but that's about to change. Any day now the silver bells, cockle shells and pretty maids all in a row will show up. What's growing in *your* garden?

8

SHADE FOR US ALL

"Then the Lord God sent a vine and made it grow up over Jonah. It gave him more shade for his head. It made him more comfortable. Jonah was very happy he had the vine." (Jonah 4:6 NIRV)

"Nothing is going to change in the Congo until you and I figure out what is wrong with the person in the mirror." (Donald Miller)

Apparently, it's considered quite the blessing to park yourself under a vine. Personally, I would take a palm tree any day, but that's me. Better yet, if someone were to invite me to take refuge in their air-conditioned condo on a hot blustery day along with some liquid refreshment, I could make myself quite comfortable.

The vine wasn't just a big overgrown bush for Jonah's comfort and enjoyment. It was an object lesson. I can just hear God saying to Jonah, "Oh, you poor, dehydrated little cactus. Let me rejuvenate you with a lovely vine!" And Jonah sighs heavily and says, "Yes, Lord. That would be nice. And maybe a leather recliner while you're at it." So, God gives him the vine and a coupon for Crate and Barrel. And Jonah was "very happy about the vine." All is well in Nineveh.

But by dawn the next day, God sent a worm to chew up the vine. And if that wasn't enough, He unleashed a scorching wind and the blazing sun. It got so hot that Jonah wanted to die. How he longed to go back to his days on the whale cruise tour ship.

Jonah didn't want God to save anyone outside his extended family and nation. What the heck was his problem? I was quick to point a finger … but that led to a finger pointing back at me. Haven't *I* been sitting under that vine at one time or another? Haven't we all? We sit smugly in our own denominations, thinking we're the only ones God approves of.

A few years ago, I had a short stint writing devotionals for our local newspaper. I thought about including my church name in my moniker, but then I realized that if I said I was Lutheran, the Catholics wouldn't read it. And if I said I was Baptist, the Methodists wouldn't read it. No matter which denomination I claimed as mine, there would always be someone who thought it was the wrong one. So, I refused to identify myself with any denomination.

How do I know that some of the denominations are exclusive in their beliefs? Because I've been there. Over the years I moved from one denomination to the next, trying to find the perfect fit. And when I was in each of those churches, I thought all the other churches were hopelessly lost. Have you ever sat under that vine?

What about *this* vine:" If some of the branches have been broken off, and you, though a wild olive shoot, have been grafted in among the others and now share in the nourishing sap from the olive root, do not consider yourself to be superior to those other branches. If you do, consider this: You do not support the root, but the root supports you" (Romans 11:17,18).

None of us planted ourselves here. I don't know about you, but I feel so darn lucky! I know, I know, luck had nothing to do with it. I'm supposed to say "blessed" instead of lucky, but "lucky" makes me feel like I just won the lottery; like the best thing in the whole wide world just swept me off my feet.

My grandson had a school assignment last April. He was supposed to go outside and yell "Loof Lirpa! Loof Lirpa!" until the Loof Lirpa bird appeared. In case the bird didn't appear, he was to stand in front of a mirror and yell, "Loof Lirpa," and it would most assuredly appear before his very eyes. The next day when he came home from school, I asked Wyatt what that assignment was all about, and he explained that "Loof Lirpa" is "April Fool," backwards.

I think instead of looking out for those troublesome "Loof Lirpas," we should occasionally take a good, long look in the mirror.

9

TALK TO THE HAND

"Truly I tell you, if anyone says to this mountain, 'Go, throw yourself into the sea,' and does not doubt in their heart but believes that what they say will happen, it will be done for them." (Mark 11:23)

"Seeing is not always believing." (Martin Luther King)

My neighbor Clara has a quirky habit when she's playing cards. She likes to address the cards as if they were a close bunch of relatives. As she's laying down a card she can't use, she'll say "I don't want *you*."

I guess I'm guilty of talking to inanimate objects, too. I've been known to speak to my appliances on occasion. Like the time my washing machine started wailing like a banshee. "Kwitcher caterwallin, mister!" I yelled, as I stuffed more laundry into it. Or when the toaster kept popping the bread out before it was toasted, "Turn or burn!" I'd yell, as I jammed the bread slices back down. You don't want to know what I said to the can opener.

Jesus spoke with authority to many situations while He walked the earth. He spoke to a fig tree, and it shriveled up and died. He spoke to a storm and calmed the waves. He spoke words of healing to people with diseases, and they were healed. He even sent demons into a herd of pigs and talked them over a cliff and into a lake. Those swine flew! (Pun intended).

What kinds of mountains can we speak to that need to take a nosedive? How about our financial situation— are things looking grim? We should never admit that! We are never beaten until we admit it. "If anyone speaks, they should do so as one who speaks the very words of God" (1 Peter 4:11). So, what does God's Word have to say about our finances? "And my God will meet *all* your needs according to the riches of his glory in Christ Jesus" (Phil 4:19). Since it is our faith that pleases God, why not take Him at His Word and believe for the best?

Is there anything that you're afraid of? "God didn't give us a spirit that makes us weak and fearful. He gave us a spirit that gives us power and love. It helps us control ourselves" (2 Tim 1: 7 NIRV). Remember what happened to Job when he lost it all? Later on, he admitted he was battling with fear. "What I feared has come upon me; what I dreaded has happened to me" (Job 3:25).

Anytime you start talking fear, the enemy gains a foothold into that situation. Whenever you feel fear rising up, stuff it back down where it came from and start responding in faith. "I can do all this through him who gives me strength" (Phil 4:13). "For we live by faith, not by sight" (2 Cor 5:7).

Our words are powerful. God created the world with His spoken words, and we were made in His image. So, just like our Father, we create the world around us with our words. We might not create animals or rainbows, but certainly we can create beauty to a lesser extent, and some things we do will be even greater than the things Jesus did (John 14:12).

God designed us in such a way that our words even override our thoughts. That means that we could be thinking about one thing, but the minute we start talking about another thing, the thinking stops. That happens to me all the time! Heheh …

But don't take my word for it, try it for yourself. Start counting (silently) to 10 in your head. Go ahead; I'll wait …. Quick! Shout your favorite color out loud! Did you see what just happened? The minute you started talking, you stopped counting. You can't think one thing while you're saying another.

Here's another fun way to try this out. Go through the drive-through at McDonalds and start thinking about a Big Mac. Then when you get to the window, order a hamburger. I guarantee you're getting a hamburger. Not exactly a happy meal.

Ever hear the expression "What you see is what you get?" That's not true. What you *say* is what you get. If you want a Big Mac, then say so. And if you want a more beautiful world around you, then speak to the stumbling blocks and the washing machine and the checkbook. And don't forget to speak to that deck of cards. Talk to the hand!

10

AM I FORGETTING SOMETHING?

"Praise the LORD, my soul, and forget not all his benefits." (Psalm 103:2)

"Blessed are those who can give without remembering and take without forgetting." (Elizabeth Bibesco)

For the past few years, I've been volunteering at a nursing home. I'll never forget my first day on the job. I was lining up the residents in wheelchairs at the elevator after an afternoon of movies and popcorn, when a lovely, white-haired woman who seemed to take a liking to me requested that I take her back to her room.

So, I was standing alongside this woman while we waited for the elevator, feeling rather proud that I was handpicked for this privilege, when suddenly she turned to me and asked, "Do you live around here?" I assured her that I did. A few minutes later she turned to me again and asked if I lived around here. I said yes. Then a few minutes later … well, you can probably guess, she asked if I lived around here. Guess who didn't feel so special anymore. (I never should have told Mark about that. To this day he teases me. Whenever I forget where I put something, he'll say, "Do you live around here?")

The next weekend it was game day at the nursing home. We had fun playing a game which gave each of the residents a chance to share some of their personal stories. At one point during the game, I asked which kinds of pies were their favorites. Several of the residents piped up with "lemon meringue" and "banana cream." They looked so happy when they were thinking about their favorite pies that it really got to me. I didn't know how long it had been since they had a really good piece of pie, so I decided to bring a pie with me at some point in the near future.

The following week, we played *Outburst* in the game room. I wrote the residents answers to the questions on the chalk board. After the game ended, I erased the board and wrote down about ten different kinds of pies so we could take a vote on which pie was most popular. I told the residents that the following week I would bring in two pies from a local bakery for them to enjoy (remember, I wanted them to have "good" pie, that's why I didn't offer to make them myself).

I asked for a show of hands for each flavor pie. Hardly anyone raised their hands! Where were the folks who only a week ago had practically salivated over banana cream and lemon meringue pies? (Come on, what's your favorite kind of pie? Think man, think!)

Psalm 103:2 tells us to do two things: (1) praise the Lord, and (2) don't forget his benefits. Those two things can be summed up into one, because when you're praising God for what He has done, you're remembering.

I can be forgetful about many things, but when God does something for me, I never forget. One morning a few years ago I woke up from a dream that our mailbox was full of checks. Just then Mark woke up and said "I just dreamt our mailbox was full of checks!" When two people have the same dream at the same time, you have to admit, that's God. Mark keeps forgetting what happened that day. I don't. I write down all my dreams and conversations with God in my journal. There's not a day that goes by that I don't thank God for everything He does for us. I even thank Him for things some people take for granted, like water. I thank Him that I can shower everyday (my family thanks Him for that, too). And in thanking Him, I'm remembering His benefits.

Around the time we had those dreams, Mark was presented with a wonderful self-employment opportunity, and ever since then our mailbox *has* been full of checks. However, sometimes a few days go by with no checks, and Mark gets nervous. Crabby even. As the head of our household, I can understand why he worries about the finances, but I won't go there. I remind him that God told us the checks are in the mailbox, and unless God changes His mind and tells us otherwise, I'm going to stand on His Word.

God is more than willing to give us the desires of our heart, but He needs to hear our prayers of gratitude and remembrance all the same. Why does He need to hear all of these things? *Because we forget.*

LASSO THE MOON

"If Your Presence does not go with us, do not send us
up from here."
(Ex 33:15)

"What is it you want, Mary? What do you want? You
want the moon? Just say the word and I'll throw a lasso
around it and pull it down. Hey, that's a pretty good
idea. I'll give you the moon." (*It's a Wonderful Life*)

God's Presence went before Moses and the Israelites in the form of a cloud. I wonder what that must have been like. There have been many times I desperately needed God to reassure me that He was with me, but instead I felt strangely alone. I would show up at our meeting place with my Bible and cup of coffee, and I'd end up saying, "God? Hello? I'm here to spend time with you, are you going to show up? Otherwise, I'm just going to read this *People* magazine lying on the table. Maybe some of those skinny, size two movie stars will make me feel even crappier about myself." (That's okay. I overeat on purpose. Having a beautiful body threatens me.) Or on the bright side, maybe another celebrity is adopting a third world baby; now *that's* sure to inspire me!

I think if I would have been traveling in Moses entourage, that cloud would have driven me crazy. I would have been so paranoid that the cloud would disappear if I made the wrong turn, or if I stopped to catch some zz's that it would be gone when I awoke. I probably wouldn't have been able to keep my eyes on the road. My toes would have been covered in bandages from constantly stubbing them on rocks because I would have been so busy watching the cloud, that I wasn't watching my own feet. But Moses had more than just *following* the cloud to worry about. According to Exodus 33:3, the cloud was in danger of disappearing altogether:

God said, "Go up to the land flowing with milk and honey. But I will not go with you, because you are a stiff-necked people and I might destroy you on the way." This, after they had traded God in for a golden calf.

What in interesting offer God presents to Moses! "Go! Stuff your faces with milk and honey (modern translation—DQ Moo Lattes with extra caramel). Go, stock your garages with exotic cars, your houses with big screen TVs and Nintendos. Go, take a Caribbean cruise, wine and dine on champagne and caviar. But. I'm. Not. Going. With. You." Would you want the milk and honey without God? I wouldn't.

Sometimes when I'm sitting quietly in God's Presence, the longing to reach out and wrap my arms around Him is so intense that I can't stand it. I can't bear the thought that He would go anywhere without me. I don't know if I could lasso the moon for anyone like George offered to do, but if God was the moon I would surely try. I would don my Stetson and toss up the biggest chunk of rope I could find. I'd probably leave a cloud of dust under my heels as I got dragged along, but that's okay. I guess that's the price a desperado has to pay, but it's worth it.

Jesus had His fair share of desperados. There was Zacchaeus, who climbed a tree to get a better view of Him (Luke 19:1-8), the paralytic man who was lowered through the ceiling so Jesus would touch him (Luke 5:18-20) and the woman with the issue of blood who pushed her way through the crowd to touch Jesus' hem (Mark 5:25-34). There are many more stories in the Bible just like these; tales of faithful men and women who would have cut off their right arm just to be close to Jesus. So, you see? I'm not the only wrangler in the Wild West.

The next time you're sipping a fancy coffee drink or playing with a new-fangled gadget from Best Buy, imagine trying to enjoy it if God wasn't around. I think I could still scarf down a Moo Latte, but without God's help my flat screen TV and surround sound stereo would never make it out of the box. I'm not mechanically minded, but He is. I couldn't make a move without God, nor would I want to. Are you watching for the cloud? Oh, here it comes! Now where did I put that rope …

A FOOL FOR CHRIST

"We have been made a spectacle to the whole universe, to angels as well as to human beings. We are fools for Christ ..." (1Cor 4:9-10)

"He is not seeking a powerful people to represent Him. Rather, He looks for all those who are weak, foolish, despised, and written off: and He inhabits them with His own strength." (Graham Cooke)

I started making a fool of myself early in life. When I was in the third grade, I was sitting at my desk one day, bored and restless, when I started wondering if perhaps my foot would fit into the cubby of my desk. Yeah, it fit! It fit a little *too* well; it was stuck! So, I started rocking back and forth in an attempt to dislodge my foot, which caused my desk to fall backwards on the floor. There I was on my back, with my foot sticking straight up in the air, still wedged tightly in the desk. To make matters worse, I was wearing a skirt that day, so the whole class had a pretty good view of my underwear.

My mother always warned me to wear my nicest underwear in public in case I should meet with an unfortunate accident. I don't remember what condition my underwear was in that day, but suffice it to say, wearing hand-me-downs from my four older sisters had put me in quite the awkward position.

I think the question isn't so much have I been a fool all along, but am I willing to become a fool for Christ? I suppose if I were highly intelligent to begin with, it might cause me some embarrassment to become a fool. But if I've been a fool all my life, what do I have to lose?

Let's face it. He's God, and we're … not. I imagine to a Maker who loads the skies with a smathering of stars, swirls the clouds with His Hand and parts a massive body of water like it's just another play day in the bathtub, to Him, driving cars, flying airplanes and building skyscrapers is child's play. "For the foolishness of God is wiser than human wisdom, and the weakness of God is stronger than human strength" (1 Cor 1:25). But still, He peers down through the clouds to get a glimpse of us, captivated by our antics (Psalm 113:6).

So, I'm a fool for Christ. And so are you. If we thought we were so smart, or "all that," God would have no use for us. As it stands, He can do quite a bit with our foolishness. "Brothers and sisters, think of what you were when you were called. Not many of you were wise by human standards; not many were influential; not many were of noble birth. But God chose the foolish things of the world to shame the wise; God chose the weak things of the world to shame the strong. God chose the lowly things of this world and the despised things—and the things that are not—to nullify the things that are, so that no one may boast before him" (1 Cor 1:26-29).

God tends to choose the foolish among us instead of the gifted or talented. The foolish realize that they are most undeserving and have fully embraced the fact that without Him they are not qualified. Those who lean on Him completely know that within themselves there is no good thing apart from their faith in Him.

If we're weak and foolish, that opens the door for God to be big and strong. The more we lean on God, the more He's glorified. If we start developing pride in our works, we'll end up bragging and then we'll be further away from God because we'll think we can do it all without Him. So our foolishness glorifies God! Still, some days my foolishness gets the best of me.

I'm glad God made sure to include fools in the Bible, otherwise I'd worry I was the only one. Zacchaeus climbed a sycamore tree to get a glimpse of Jesus as He walked by. He might have looked like a fool to some people, don't you think? Imagine in this day and age if the Pope was planning a parade down Hollywood Blvd, and Jay Leno climbed a palm tree to get a closer look. Fool? Big time. But in Zacchaeus' case, Jesus was so pleased with his act of desperation, He invited Himself over to Zach's house for dinner! I have done some pretty desperate things trying to get God's attention. Who knows, maybe He'll come to *my* house for dinner. I hope He likes macaroni and cheese.

If you're gonna make a fool of yourself, it might as well be over the likes of impressing God, and not your neighbor or fellow pew-warmer at church. God might smile over your antics, but the rest of the world thinks you're a dang fool!

13

YOU SAY POTATO, I SAY POTAHTO

POTATO: "I tell you, my friends, do not be afraid of those who kill the body and after that can do no more. But I will show you whom you should fear: Fear him who, after the body has been killed, has authority to throw you into hell." (Luke 12:4-6)

POTAHTO: "For the Spirit God gave us does not make us timid, but gives us power, love and self-discipline." (2 Tim 1:7)

When my grandson Wyatt was 3 years old, he experienced his first tornado warning. When the sirens went off, his eyes got as big as saucers, and he started to cry. I explained what a tornado was, and how we had to take cover in the basement. He asked me to pray for his mom and dad and friends and neighbors and pets, so I did, and that seemed to reassure him.

A few weeks later, Wyatt was playing outside when a car alarm went off. He came running into the house yelling "Grammy, pray for me! The potato is coming back!" You have to watch out for those potatoes, they can get quite large and intimidating, heheh …

In Exodus 19 and 20, God decides to put on a show for the Israelites. He warned Moses ahead of time, so the people would be prepared in advance. There was a laundry list of requirements. They had to wash their clothes, be consecrated by Moses and stay clear of the mountain until they heard the ram's horn sound off. If anyone tried to climb the mountain or even touch it without following these rules, they would die.

Exodus 20:15-19 describes the scene: "When the people saw the thunder and lightning and heard the trumpet and saw the mountain in smoke, they trembled with fear. They stayed at a distance and said to Moses, 'Speak to us yourself and we will listen. But do not have God speak to us or we will die.'"

My first impression of this event was, "Come on, you wusses! How many times has God offered to light up His Holy mountain for you?" I mean, here was their chance to meet with God Face to face! But then reality settled in. They were in the eye of the potato. It was a good thing *I* wasn't there. Like a fool I would have started running up the mountain, and God would have killed me. This old potato would have been an order of fries in a flash of lightning. Still, what a way to go!

Moses reassured the people, "Do not be afraid. God has come to test you, so that the fear of God will be with you to keep you from sinning." God wanted them to fear Him for their own good; not just to scare them silly for the fun of it. But I suspect God wanted even more than that.

See, I really believe that I could have gone up that mountain and lived to tell about it, like Moses did. Maybe that's because I have a different kind of fear towards God. My fear is more like this: "The fear of the LORD is the beginning of wisdom, and knowledge of the Holy One is understanding." (Proverbs 9:10)

My knowledge of God may only amount to a hill of beans, but I love Him too much to be afraid of Him. Don't misunderstand, I respect and revere Him. I mean, come on, He's God! But my understanding of Him is that He's a God of love, and I have experienced that love too many times to be afraid of Him. There is no fear in love (1 John 4:18).

So, there appears to be two kinds of fear mentioned in the Bible. The first kind is a dreadful potato fear, the kind the Israelites felt that day at the mountain. The second kind is the potahto fear that goes hand in hand with wisdom and the knowledge of God's love.

These two types of fear were in the world as early as the Garden of Eden. Adam and Eve first experienced the potahto kind of fear. They loved and trusted God with affectionate reverence. But after they succumbed to temptation, the potato kind of fear set in. Guilt and shame took up residence on that day. They had lost the intimate relationship they had with God, and a dreadful fear replaced their reverence. God didn't change, but their perception of Him did.

I'm going to take Moses' advice and not be afraid. God's intention isn't to kill us; it's to keep us from sin. And even more importantly, it's to help us step into our roles as sons and daughters of the King, to revere and love our Heavenly Father. As for those potatoes, I'll probably find myself running if I ever see *them* raining down from the sky. I'm on a low-carb diet.

But potatoes, French fries and other carbohydrates aside, I guess it all boils down to this: Do we perceive

God to be a big fist in the sky, waiting to clobber us, or do we have a sense of wonder toward the universe, looking at the stars and moon, and exclaiming, "My Daddy made that!" *Who's your Daddy?*

BIRDCAGE BLUES

"See how the farmer waits for the land to yield its valuable crop, patiently waiting for the autumn and spring rains." (James 5:7)

"He who sows hurry reaps indigestion." (Robert Louis Stevenson)

I love that scripture. Whenever I struggle with patience, I just picture a farmer who plants his crop and then, hands on hips, hollers at the seeds to hurry up and grow. He could yell until he's blue in the face, but those seeds won't grow any faster. No, he goes about his business until it's harvest time. Farmers must have more patience than saints.

Last spring, we took our grandkids to California. We decided to take the Mulholland Scenic Parkway in Los Angeles for some breathtaking vistas before we headed to our final destination of Disneyland. Not a great idea. We got stuck in traffic for hours. Our grandkids never experienced traffic of this magnitude before. The longest they ever sat in a car to get from one place to another was 20 minutes. Wyatt was beside himself with frustration. His cries went from, "Are we there yet?" to "Get me outta here!"

After we had been sitting in one place for over two hours, our daughter Jenni called to see how it was going (or in our case, how it *wasn't* going). Wyatt wanted to talk to her, so I handed him the phone.

"Aunt Jenni!" he yelled. "We've been sitting here all day! Can you call the people in these cars and tell them to move?!"

"I don't know their phone numbers, Wyatt." Jenni said.

We were all howling with laughter by that point. Well, all except for Wyatt. He was in tears; a very difficult day for a boy impatient to get to Disneyland. We tried to get Wyatt's mind off of the situation by playing the "happy" game—thanking God for all the things He has done for us; sunny skies, a great vacation, we're all safe and healthy, but Wyatt was beyond consolation.

It's easy to have patience when everything is going our way; when our schedule runs smoothly, when nothing spontaneous interrupts without our permission or when traffic moves along to our liking. But when the cage door slams shut, we become prisoners of futility, and futility always ruffles our feathers. The prison bars are all around us, but the real trap is within. In most cases we are the cause of our own suffering.

Instead of beating a spoon against the prison bars, what if we use this time of imprisonment to develop patience? It's one of the fruits of the Spirit (Gal 5:22-23). It seems the best way to develop this particular fruit is to be trapped somewhere. Your reaction is a good gauge to see where you're at with the patience barometer.

The word *patience* is derived from the Latin word "pati," which means to suffer, endure or bear. Suffering without complaining takes practice. God knows that. That's why he lets us sit and stew in rush hour traffic and puts us in grocery lines behind people with coupons, screaming babies, and the slow moving hoi polloi. Suffering in silence will feel repugnant at first, even against the very forces of nature, but after the first hundred jail sentences it will be a cakewalk. I can't think of a better spiritual growth opportunity.

What will we get for all this prison time? We peek out between the bars to see if God is anywhere in sight. Will he pull a "Beam me up Scotty" and get us out of gridlock traffic or long lines? Probably not, but He will reward us with more grace and refine us more golden than a crop of corn if we pass the patience test.

So, the next time you start to feel like a jail bird waiting for parole, use that time of frustration to play the "happy" game. Can you walk? See? Hear? Feed yourself? Is there food on your table? A roof over your head? Great. You have more than two thirds of the world's population does. And if that doesn't do it for you, remind yourself that Jesus didn't complain when they spat at Him, whipped Him and hung Him on a cross. If He was able to endure all that suffering in silence, surely, we can hold our tongues and keep our cool when things aren't going our way.

You now have the key to open the door of your birdcage. Hang on to that. You'll be locked up a few more times before you finally learn to fly.

15

THE FLAG LADY

"If they keep quiet, the stones will cry out." (Luke 19:40)

"Those who danced were thought to be quite insane by those who could not hear the music." (Angela Monet)

Several years ago, I attended a Christian conference in Nashville, where I encountered a precious saint whom I affectionately dubbed "the flag lady." The flag lady was animated in her worship to the Lord. She would run to the altar wildly waving her flag, and then dance at the altar. Trouble was, in her exuberance she would accidentally hit the other worshipers in the head with her flag. I took a liking to this obnoxious flag-yielding woman. She was so innocent in her worshipful prancing and her love for the Lord.

When it was time for the guest speaker to preach, the flag lady took a seat right next to me. My friend took out a box of cinnamon Altoid mints and offered some to us. Have you ever had a cinnamon Altoid? It's a very strong breath freshener—so powerful and bold that they make your eyes water and your mouth feel as though it were on fire.

I took one, and then held out the box to the flag lady. Surprisingly, she reached into the box and grabbed a large handful of Altoids, tossed the whole fistful of mints into her mouth, and then proceeded to chomp them down like they were M&M's! I'm sorry, but I lost it at that point. I was laughing so much throughout the rest of the sermon that people started to wonder if I was drunk in the spirit.

The flag lady reminded me of David. 2 Samuel 6 tells the story of David leading a procession of people with the Ark of the Lord, dancing with all his might. I wonder if his dance moves resembled the jitterbug or the twist, or if he cut a rug in his own unique style, with a passion. Dancing in the Old Testament times was probably a very rigid and formal affair, something along these lines: "Thou shalt put thy right foot in, put thy right foot out, put thy right foot in and thus shake it all about." But Daniel broke all the rules and worshiped with reckless abandon.

Does worshiping God require a passionate action such as David's? What about people with reserved personalities? The ones who don't scream their heads off at football games, or jump wildly up and down during Sunday morning worship? I mean, do we have to thrash our bodies about to prove how much we love God? In a word … no.

God can be worshiped in many ways; singing, shouting, enjoying God in nature, kneeling in reverence during a church service, or studying God's word are just an example of the ways we can worship Him, based on our own backgrounds and God-given personalities. For the flag ladies of the world, their demonstration of loving God involves using every body part, but a simple act of obedience speaks just as loudly to God of our devotion.

The main thing to remember when your feet hit the floor, is to be sincere in your worship. Are you feeling over the top in your spirit like David did? Then go with that. Are you feeling peaceful and mellow in your spirit? Never allow anyone to marsh your mellow. Just be sincere in your worship, and don't let what anyone else thinks control your groove moves for the Lord.

I imagine God gets to gander at a wide variety of worship styles from heaven. Personally, I'm not the shouting, contortionist type. But if I were to cavort myself around, I'd be a little worried about how my dancing technique would look to Him. My two left feet and offbeat rhythm might cause Him to chuckle, but as long as I put my heart and soul into it, I know it will please Him. Does anyone have a flag I can borrow?

16

BELLS AND WHISTLES

"How faint the whisper we hear of Him! Who then can understand the thunder of His power?" (Job 26:14)

"We need to find God, and He cannot be found in noise and restlessness. God is the friend of silence. See how nature, trees, flowers, grass grows in silence; see the stars, the moon and the sun, how they move in silence. We need silence to be able to touch souls.
(Mother Teresa)

There is so much noise inside my head these days, I can barely stand it. Beeps and buzzers, bells and whistles. I'm not stark-raving mad (well, maybe I am, what do I know). I'm talking about the fanfare of telephones ringing, microwaves beeping, doorbells clanging and car horns blasting. A million angels just got their wings.

We're programmed early on in life to jump when the bell rings (you can blame that on Pavlov). Take the ice cream truck, for example, blaring annoying music as it crusades down the street. Children come running out of their houses as the Pied Piper lures them into his snare. When my kids were little and the ice cream truck drove past playing their music, I would tell them, "That's the song they play when they're *out* of ice cream."

Several evangelists come to mind on the subject of noise. They walk out to the podium and immediately launch into World War III: "GAWD IS IN DA HOUSE!" they'll yell, as they pace back and forth on the stage "AND GAAWWD ISN'T AFRAID OF THE DEVIL!" Then they stomp their feet and thump their Bibles for added effect.

And then you have the people that are hand talkers. They think their voice alone isn't enough, so they start flapping their hand signals to get the job done. Mark is one of those hand people. He literally cannot talk unless he's using his hands! Once, when we were driving down the highway, I reached over to hold his hand. To my surprise, he actually took his other hand off the wheel in order to continue his conversation. "Look Ma, no hands!"

Now if only God would speak to us this loudly, we wouldn't have any excuses for ignoring Him. Though there are times He will shout to get our attention, most of the time He whispers ever so quietly, gentleman that He is. Instead of zapping lightning bolts to get our cooperation, He walks softly and carries a big Bible.

The Lord said, "Go out and stand on the mountain in the presence of the LORD, for the LORD is about to pass by." Then a great and powerful wind tore the mountains apart and shattered the rocks before the LORD, but the LORD was not in the wind. After the wind there was an earthquake, but the LORD was not in the earthquake. After the earthquake came a fire, but the LORD was not in the fire. *And after the fire came a gentle whisper* (1 Kings 19:11-13).

I was never any good at "telephone" back in the day. Remember that game? You had to whisper in someone's ear, and the message got passed along until the last kid in line repeated what he heard. What started out as, "Your pants are on fire" could end up as "Your aunt smokes cigars." Just my luck I'll get the message jumbled when God starts whispering in my ear.

I once asked Mark if he was glad I didn't play any

guessing games with him. If I want something, I come right out and say it. To which he replied, "I just do whatever the voices in your head tell me to."

If we don't calm down and spend some time sitting quietly in God's presence, we might miss His whisper. Sometimes it's in the silence that He speaks the loudest.

17

THE TALE OF THE GOLDEN COW

"So I gave them over to their stubborn hearts to follow their own devices." (Ps 81:12)

"Waiting is one of life's hardships." (Lemony Snicket)

I laugh every time this memory comes to mind. Last summer we made a last-minute decision to go camping. The trailer was parked in the driveway, and I had taken our dog Otis with me to run a few errands. When I got home, I backed the truck into the driveway so it would be ready to hook up to the trailer, even though we weren't leaving for a few more hours. When I walked over to the passenger side and opened the door, Otis refused to get out.

He wasn't stupid, he had seen the trailer. He knows the trailer means we're going camping, a sheer delight for any dog who's an avid hunter and nature lover. He gets nervous when he sees the trailer because he worries that we'll leave without him.

He sat there stiff as a statue, looking straight ahead, pretending he couldn't hear me saying, "Otis, come!" He was afraid that if he got out we would leave without him, so he continued to stare straight ahead, as if to say, "I can't see you, and I can't hear you." Eventually I had to pick him up and carry him out.

I learned something about myself that day. I saw my own stubborn, strong-willed heart that so many times in the past had deceived me into thinking I had to grab on to things with a vice-like grip and hang on for dear life, instead of placing that desire at God's feet and trusting Him to supply all my needs.

There was a hilarious episode of the Andy Griffith show that dealt with this very subject. The townspeople had just come from church where they heard an inspirational sermon about slowing down and not rushing through life. They took that sermon to heart and retreated to Andy's porch where they rested and drank soda pop. Then someone started reminiscing about the town band they used to have, and just like that they decided to have a concert that very evening.

So, they're suddenly up and running to patch up their old band uniforms and rebuild the platform, hoping to put on a concert by nightfall. But by the end of the day, they find themselves back on Andy's porch, exhausted from the day's activities, and realizing the irony of their futility. Just then the pastor came walking by and commented on how nice and relaxed everyone looked.

In Exodus 32, the Israelites did the same thing as the Andy Griffians. They decided they wanted something (a god) instantly, so instead of waiting on the real God, they went ahead and made their own god in the likeness of a golden cow. I don't know about you, but when I'm looking for a little heavenly intervention, I don't want to go looking for it in a cow pasture.

If we're not careful with our hastiness, God might give us over to our own devices (Romans 1:24). Instant gratification leads to a wild goose chase, which winds up in a dumpster of misguided appetites and ill-conceived passions. And even though God is good and tired of the garbage heap of our gluttony, He'll let us wallow in it a little more, until the stench becomes overpowering. Truthfully, I'm in need of a little fresh air around here. Seriously, something stinks to high heaven. (Note to self: change socks daily.)

God isn't slow to answer our prayers. Sometimes His answer to our prayer is "no," sometimes it's "yes," and other times it's "yes, in a little while." Our impatience can cause us to take the second kind of "yes" to mean "no." We're like those kids riding in the car with their parents, asking "Are we there yet? Are we there yet? Are we there yet?" We must drive God absolutely crazy sometimes. We're always in a hurry, but it seems like He never is.

If you're impatient and always in a hurry like me, try this good old-fashioned litmus test: How many licks does it take to get to the center of a Tootsie Pop? The temptation to bite into the Tootsie Pop is too great an act of patience for many a man and owl. When you have conscientiously licked your Tootsie Pop one lick at a time to its center, then and only then will you be able to abstain from those impulsive deeds that have plagued mankind since the creation of time. Here we go … ah-one, ta-whoo, tha-ree-hee …

18

THE COOKIE MONSTER

"There is no fear in love." (1 John 4:18)

"Me want cookies." (The Cookie Monster)

My dad had a hard childhood and life, and because he never was given love, he didn't know how to give it. I don't remember ever feeling loved by him when I was a kid. He complained many times about what a burden we all were, and in order to keep from upsetting him, we had to be quiet as a mouse when he was around. The only emotion I had toward him was fear.

But yet, there were times when Dad would show me affection. If he was in a good mood and things were going his way, he would pat me on the head and give me a cookie or a candy bar. This was the only way he knew how to show love. Years of showing *myself* love in this way has taken its toll in an accumulation of weight from too many peanut butter cups and sugar cookies. (I'm not fat, just gravity enhanced.)

One childhood memory in particular has been etched into my memory. It was Christmas, and my sisters and I were having fun decorating Christmas cookies. We were competing to see who could produce the most beautiful cookie. And then Dad came in and hollered at us for making a mess and sent us to our rooms.

When my kids baked cookies, I brought out tons of colored sugars and sprinkles and let them make as big a mess as they want. In fact, their artwork was so amazing that I started an online bakery. But later I accidentally deleted all my cookies.

A few years ago, at a Christian conference, I was up at the altar during worship time, when I had a vision. I was suddenly standing before God's throne. I opened up my right hand, and it was full of sprinkles. The sprinkles started going up and circling God's throne.

Then I opened up my left hand, and it was full of colored glitter, and the glitter rose up and circled around God, too, until there was a beautiful rainbow of colors decorating His throne. Then I realized I was empty handed and had nothing left to give Him, when He said, "Give me your cookies."

At that point I thought I must be getting hungry and imagining the whole thing. But He said it again. "Give me your cookies." I suddenly realized that God was showing me that He loved my artwork, and He was decorating His Throne with it!

In his old age, Dad moved into a nursing home, where I visited him several times a week. I always stopped at the gift shop first to buy him a molasses cookie (those were his favorite). I wasn't actually allowed to give him any sweets, because he was diabetic. But day after day he would sit in his tiny, joyless room with nothing to look forward to, so the cookies were our little secret.

One day right after handing him his cookie, the nurse walked in! In a panic, I quickly grabbed the cookie out of his mouth and flung it across the room, which left him looking quite bewildered. After the nurse left, I gave it back to him, explaining that he wasn't allowed to eat cookies.

When I left that day, the nurse came back in, and I looked back to wave goodbye to Dad. To my chagrin his lap was full of cookie crumbs! Oh dear …

The last time I visited Dad before he passed away, I gave him a hug and kiss. His skin was paper thin, and I noticed for the first time how frail he looked. He had become a skeleton of a man.

Where was the monster that had terrified me all those years? He hugged me back and told me he loved me. Never in my life had he said that to me without me saying it first. I asked if I could bring him something the next time, and he said, "I don't need anything. All I need is your love." (Wow!)

God had given me a beautiful memory to replace all the bad ones. Not only did he soften Dad's heart so he could love, but God showed me that HIS all-consuming love had been there all along.

Oh yeah, one more thing. Someday when I'm old and sitting in a nursing home somewhere ... for the love of God, LET ME HAVE A COOKIE!

God has been watching over you since you were a child, taking great delight in all your works of art. He still is.

19

TWO CAN PLAY THIS GAME

"The husband should fulfill his marital duty to his wife, and likewise the wife to her husband." (1Cor 7:3)

"I was married by a judge. I should have asked for a jury." (Groucho Marx)

My marriage is in trouble. It all started a few years ago, when I drifted away from … Diet Coke. Mark and I were both in it for the long haul with our addiction to Diet Coke. But one day at a fast-food restaurant I was forced to drink Diet Pepsi because they didn't have Coke products ... and I liked it! Now *this* was the real thing! The war was on.

Depending on who's doing the shopping, our refrigerator is either stocked with Coke or Pepsi products. I know it probably sounds selfish of me to keep bringing Pepsi home, but since Mark doesn't have a clue what's good for him, and I do, I have to make these tough decisions myself. I'm just taking care of my man! After all, have I not been ordained the "helper" in the following scripture? "It is not good for the man to be alone. I will make a helper suitable for him" (Gen 2:18).

Some people read that and put the woman in her place, tout de suite. She's supposed to be barefoot and pregnant, and work like a slave doing laundry, cooking and cleaning, right? Wait a New York minute! Isn't the husband expected to help out once in a while too? A healthy marriage takes two helpers (as long as one of the two isn't Hamburger Helper).

The dictionary's definition of helper: *an extra locomotive attached to a train at the front, middle, or rear, to provide extra power for climbing a steep grade.*

I'm sorry, but I'm too weak and fragile to be pushing a locomotive around. That sounds like a job for a man. So just what is the husband supposed to do?

"Husbands, in the same way be considerate as you live with your wives and treat them with respect as the weaker partner and as heirs with you of the gracious gift of life, so that nothing will hinder your prayers" (1 Peter 3:7).

A wise mentor once said that a husband is like the soldier at the front line of war. He shoulders the brunt of the battle, protecting his wife and keeping her safe. Isn't that beautiful? Here's a mental picture to drive home the point: the next time we go camping, I'll make Mark take off his shirt and forge his way through the woods ahead of me, so the mosquitos never make it past the front line. Hey, I warned you it was a *mental* picture!

Here's an even better picture of the servant husband, right out of the Bible. As Jesus was making preparations for the last supper, He instructed Peter and John to look for the man carrying a jar of water and ask if they could use the man's upper room for the Passover (Luke 22:10). My NIV study notes say: "*It was extraordinary to see a man carrying a jar of water, since this was normally woman's work.*" Guess what? This was the man Jesus chose to host His dinner party.

Even in modern day America, we find it extraordinary to see men doing women's work. There are still lots of men in my family alone who fill their bellies at Thanksgiving, and then retreat to the den to watch football, leaving the women (who cooked the meal) to clean up the mess afterward. There is only one man in my family who you will find carrying dirty dishes to the sink, and that would be my husband, the official postmodern water jar carrier.

So, there you have it. The evidence is in. The husband and wife are to serve each other. How's your marriage? Is it all give and take, with more taking than giving? God can bring balance to that equation, but He might be expecting a little help on your part. You be nice and help your mate! That's what I had to do. But don't make me give up my Diet Pepsi. Anything but that!

20

THESE BOOTS WERE MADE FOR WALKING

"If people do not welcome you, leave their town and shake the dust off your feet as a testimony against them." (Luke 9:5)

"The highest form of ignorance is when you reject something you don't know anything about."
(Wayne Dyer)

My earliest recollection of rejection occurred in kindergarten. I was walking to school one day, when some kids started teasing me about what I was wearing. My family wasn't well off, so whatever I was wearing that day was either a hand-me-down from my older sisters, or it came from a thrift store. I was so crushed by the taunting, that I ran back home and refused to go back to school.

When I came crying back into the house and my older brother heard my tragic story, he promised he would buy me a big bag of M&Ms if I would put on a brave face and go back to school, so I did. Who can resist M&Ms? I would have walked to the ends of the earth for these colorful candies. But what my brother failed to tell me was that I would have to share my M&Ms. Did you know that one bag of M&Ms divided between me and my eight brothers and sisters comes down to 27.5 M&Ms apiece? Hmph.

Even Jesus suffered rejection. After teaching in the synagogue one day, the crowd asked "Isn't this the carpenter? Isn't this Mary's son and the brother of James, Joseph, Judas and Simon? Aren't his sisters here with us?" And they took offense at him (Mark 6:3).

Well, look at that! They were offended by His heritage. I guess they didn't think *He* was born in the right family, either. Do you think He went running back home when they mocked Him? Well, they didn't have

M&Ms back in the day, otherwise I suspect He may have been tempted to. But they did have figs. Who could resist a good fig? Dang, by now He was probably sorry He dried up that fig tree.

Rejection had its way with me once again when I started evangelizing. If someone I had given a Bible tract to looked at me with contempt, I would walk away instead of sticking around and making a stronger argument. "Talk to the boot!" What I really wanted to do was give *them* the boot. Yeah. I'm outta here.

How did Jesus respond to rejection? I found the answer in Luke 9:51-56. Jesus was rejected by the Samaritans while making His way through their village enroute to Jerusalem. His disciples James and John (aka Sons of Thunder) asked Jesus if He wanted them to call down fire from heaven and destroy the people, but Jesus opted to hold His peace rather than strike back in vengeance. He didn't wallow in the pain of His rejection, instead He moved past that in order to deal with the hurt of those who had rejected Him. Jesus strapped on his walking boots, not His butt-kicking boots.

Luke 24:13-35 tells the story of a different kind of boot-walking excursion. The newly resurrected Jesus joined two men who were walking down the road to Emmaus. As they approached the village, Jesus acted as if He was going farther, but they urged Him to stay, so

He did. Had they not begged Him to stay, *He would have kept walking*. I like that dignified approach. Jesus never forces Himself on anyone, so why should we?

So, God was saying it's okay to shake the dust off my boots and keep walking. I guess in some ways, Jesus is just like the rest of us. He wants to be loved and needed without begging for it. Isn't that what we all want? That, and a big bag of M&Ms.

21

IF I ONLY HAD A BRAIN

"I praise you, Father, Lord of heaven and earth, because you have hidden these things from the wise and learned, and revealed them to little children." (Matt 11:25)

"Some people without brains do an awful lot of talking." (The Scarecrow, Wizard of Oz)

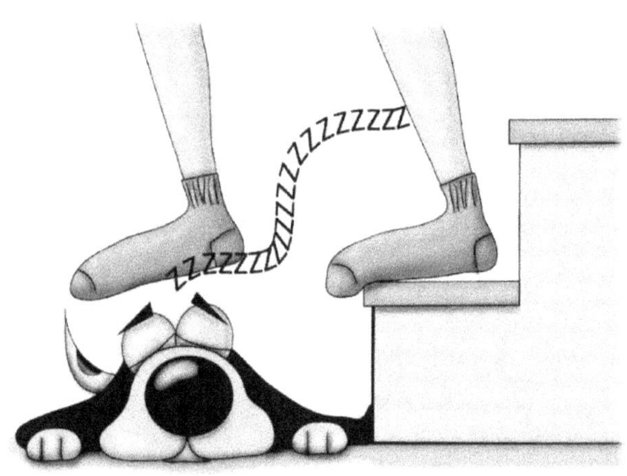

I once asked God why it is that some people have dreams and visions and see more spiritual manifestations than others do. I didn't have to wait very long to find out. One night I awoke from sleep to these words: *"You will know more about glorious manifestations if you are sur right."*

I knew this was a message from God, and I love a good game, so I donned my bathrobe and ran down the steps two at a time to look up *sur right* in the dictionary. As luck would have it, I tripped over my dog who was lying in a coma at the bottom of the steps. Poor, unsuspecting Otis. From the look on his face, I guessed he didn't appreciate playing games in the middle of the night any more than I did. God must have a different way of playing the game of *Jeopardy*. 'What is—midnight madness?'

Here's what I found for *sur right*. "Sur" means "in addition to," and "right" means just what it says—being right, or righteous. So, I think God is saying that those who are righteous +… (fill in the blank) will witness His manifestations. The Pharisees were righteous, but they were so bent on the letter of the law that they didn't recognize Jesus. To me the "+" means knowing Jesus beyond the law; desiring to know Him as much as is humanly possible. If you don't know Him beyond the law, then to you a supernatural manifestation might not be recognizable as anything that could be from Him.

Right on the heels of that discovery, I learned in the book *The Seven Mountain Prophecy* by Johnny Enlow that the left brain and right brain have two entirely different functions. The left-brain processes information logically and analytically, and the right brain processes information organically; through touching, feeling and visuals.

Jesus came into a left-brain culture with a right brain message, that's why He spoke in parables and told stories. His call to repent was a call to change our thinking habits. Repent is taken from the Greek word *metanoeo* which means "to change your mind or to think differently." Our brain is getting in the way of our heart. In order to go deeper with God, we must utilize the right side of our brain and "get the picture."

I started doing research on the internet to learn more about the left brain vs. right brain thinking patterns, and I stumbled upon a true story of a scientist named Jill Bolte Taylor who had been studying brain patterns, when one day she had a massive stroke in the left side of her brain and had only the right side of her brain to work with.

Jill described having use of only the right side of her brain as "euphoria." She fully recovered from the stroke, and now believes that people can purposefully choose to step to the right side of their brain's hemisphere. This testimony paints a pretty good picture of what life looks like on the "right" side. You can view the video of Jill's story at Ted.com.

Why do children believe in Santa Claus? They're thinking with their right brains. The idea of a big jolly man who travels all over the world via flying reindeer on Christmas Eve can only be visualized and nurtured by a right-brain thinker. Later, as the child has a few years of school under his belt in which he is taught to think logically with left-brain thinking, the idea of Santa becomes preposterous (contrary to nature, reason or common sense).

I think it's time to bring out the kid in you. Let your imagination run wild and listen for the Holy Spirit to speak to you in new ways. I don't know about you, but I'm suddenly craving milk and cookies, and a good dose of cartoons.

22

THIS IS FOR THE BIRDS!

"Look at the birds of the air; they do not sow or reap or store away in barns, and yet your heavenly Father feeds them." (Matt 6:26)

"God gives every bird its food, but He does not throw it into its nest." (J.G. Holland)

The other day Mark and I went to Perkins for breakfast. When we sat down and looked at the menu, I nearly jumped out of my seat. Peach muffins were back! I wait all year long for Perkins peach muffins. Mmmm …. I'm sitting here drooling just thinking about it. Ahhwoaeitsljkrisoohhl … (That's my Homer Simpson impression). After we finished eating, I asked our waitress to bring me a six-pack of peach muffins to take home. (Oh, I have it so bad!)

Mark immediately made a fuss about it. "What do you need six of them for? Why don't you get three peach muffins for yourself, and three raspberry muffins for me?"

"Three peach muffins?!" I sputtered. "No way! Let me have my six, and you can get six of the raspberry."

"No," he insisted, "you don't need six muffins to eat on the beach."

"What?" Where does he get off ... "I am *not* going to eat my muffins on the beach!" which caused him to laugh, explaining that he actually said, "You don't need all your muffins to be 'peach.' Okay, that was worth a good belly laugh. But I still didn't get my six peach muffins. It's high noon somewhere.

It's all my parents' fault. They instilled the pack rat mentality in all nine of us children. They grew up in poverty, and they had this deep-seated fear that one day they would run out of something, so they made sure they had an abundance of everything. There were so many cans and boxes of food and roll upon roll of paper towels and toilet paper in our basement, we could hardly make our way through it, much less find what we were sent down there to get.

I guess I brought the pack rat mentality into my marriage. Back in the day of the Y2K scare, I started saving empty milk jugs and filled them up with tap water. Before Y2K even got here the water had turned into pools of bacteria. Something good came out of that scare, though. In January 2000 all the Y2K books at Barnes and Noble were on sale for one cent! I decided not to stockpile those, though they would have been good kindling for campfires.

Exodus 16 tells the gluttonous story of the time God sent down manna from heaven for the Israelites. Moses said to them, "No one is to keep any of it until morning." However, some of them paid no attention to Moses; they kept part of it until morning, but it was full of maggots and began to smell. So, Moses was angry with them" (Ex 16:19,20).

I can just picture myself in that desert. I'd be loading up on the manna like there was no tomorrow. God taps me on the shoulder, "Uh, Deb? What's the big idea of stuffing all that manna into your purse? "And I would reply "Do you have any idea how much manna teenagers can eat?"

When Jesus sent His disciples out to preach the good news, He told them to go with just the shirts on their backs (Luke 9:1-6). No overnight bags, no food or money, not even an extra tunic. What's that, like underwear? Man, talk about feeling unclean! And when they came back, He asked them, "When I sent you without food, backpacks or Fruit of the Loom, did you lack anything?"

"Nothing," they answered. (Luke 22:35).

Do we really believe God will provide for our needs? And does Jesus' promise that He will take care of us like He does for the birds have any merit in a time of crisis? I think so. Those birds don't depend on Walmart or a local bank for their well-being. They have no clue what tomorrow will bring, nor do they fret about it.

All it takes to trust in God for our needs is a little bit of faith, and a lot of hope. Maybe throw in a bunch of coupons for good measure. And if, at any time you start to feel worried about what tomorrow will bring, just remind yourself "This is for the birds!"

23

DYING TO LIVE

"For whoever wants to save their life will lose it, but whoever loses their life for me will find it."
(Matt 16:25)

"They might tell you you're on a non-stop flight. Well, I don't think I care for that. No, I insist that my flight stop! Preferably at an airport." (George Carlin)

Someone once said that airplanes are a safer means of travel than cars. I'd have to agree with that. I like to get behind the wheel of my Ford F150 and barrel down the highway like I'm driving an ambulance. I have no problem with airplanes; after all, they *are* the safest way to fly.

I was in an airplane once that experienced turbulence so jolting, the plastic window shades slammed shut and the flight attendants were knocked to the floor. The passengers started screaming, thinking we were plunging to our death.

I calmly asked Mark to get my jacket out of the overhead bin. He asked what I wanted it for, and I said, "In case we crash, I might get cold." The passengers sitting next to us started laughing. I was glad I could offer some respite from the otherwise dire situation we were possibly facing. But the truth is I was more worried about the minutes leading up to my death, than death itself.

I even went skydiving a few years ago, jumping out of a perfectly good airplane just to prove that I had no fear. When you jump out of the plane, you lurch upwards, unfortunately not high enough to get back in the plane. And then you start falling to the earth. You'd be surprised at how something as simple as pulling a cord can be a real challenge while you're plummeting 10,000 feet to the ground. All the while I was streaking toward the earth, I tried to grab a bird to hang on to, but gravity would eventually win.

Am I a fatalist? Not really. I'm just acknowledging Who is really in charge of my life … this body. If God is in charge, and I trust Him with my life, then I should trust Him with my death. As a follower of Christ, I know that the death of my physical body just means that my spirit will live on in eternity in Christ. "For we know that if the earthly tent we live in is destroyed, we have a building from God, an eternal house in heaven, not built by human hands" (2 Cor 5:1).

We don't have the luxury of choosing how or when we die (unless we take matters into our own hands), just like we didn't have a say in when or where we would be born. Personally, I would rather go in a plane crash than to die a slow painful death from some hideous disease. But how I would go about making that happen is out of my hands. I suppose I could just book hundreds of flights once I get to the point where I'm wearing Depends and hope for the best.

I know I'm not the only one who thinks about the afterlife when traveling by airplane. The thoughts of eternity go through many people's minds the minute the wheels leave the ground. Flying thousands of feet above the earth gives one an opportunity to reflect on the possibility that in just a few minutes time your earthly life could come to an abrupt halt. Where would your soul go if your plane crashed? Do you have the peaceful assurance of knowing where you will spend eternity?

Even if we have the blessed assurance that we'll bypass hell and go straight to heaven, there still remains the element of the unknown. The Bible doesn't really give any clear-cut answers to what heaven will be like. We'll have new bodies, but it sounds like we'll still look the same as we do down here. I guess God, in His infinite wisdom, decided against giving us the option of a new look, otherwise there would have been a stampede of women lining up to get Angelina Jolie's face.

Another unknown in heaven, is what will we be doing? Personally, I was picturing myself sitting on a cloud eating chocolates and watching reruns of "Days of Our Lives." But from the looks of Revelation 11 where John is instructed to measure the temple, it looks like we might be kept rather busy up there.

God said there will be many rooms in heaven (John 14:2), but that doesn't sound reassuring to me. What kind of room will I have? Can I have a fireplace in mine? Will there be pizza? I don't see how I could possibly be happy without pizza. And do I really have to wear a robe? I'd be much more comfortable in jeans and a T-shirt.

The next time you board a plane, keep in mind that at any given moment, the destination you end up at might not be the one you had in mind should the plane land sooner than you expected it to. Do you know where *you're* going? Better pack a nice warm jacket just in case. Well, unless you plan on heading south after the crash. In that case, you might want to smuggle some ice cubes from the flight attendant's serving cart on your way down.

24

THE FALL OF WOMAN

"Then the eyes of both of them were opened, and they realized they were naked; so they sewed fig leaves together and made coverings for themselves." (Gen 3:7)

"Society is a masked ball, where everyone hides his real character, and reveals it by hiding."
(Ralph Waldo Emerson)

A while back I suffered an unfortunate accident. I fell and broke my ankle. And if that wasn't bad enough, while I was still recuperating, I fell down a flight of steps with my crutches, landing right on my already broken ankle. Those crutches are some complicated pendulums. I immediately started to cry. Loudly. But then it hit me—I'm home alone! What's the use of howling at the top of my lungs when there's nobody around to hear me? It's sort of like when a tree falls.

I crawled back up the stairs to phone Mark to take me to the hospital. My ankle had already swelled up like a balloon, and the pain was back with a vengeance. Mark yelled at me all the way to the hospital.

Lying on the bed in the ER, I suddenly noticed that something stunk. Wait a minute; I took a shower that morning, what's up with the reekage? And then I remembered I forgot to put on deodorant after my shower. I begged Mark to go back home and get it, but he wouldn't. "What are you worried about that for?" He retorted. "Come on!" I pleaded. "I can't be lying here stinking all day!" Ah, it was no use. Vanity, vanity ...

By this time the drugs started kicking in, and I was feeling no pain—literally! I had hijacked the emergency room and subjected the nurses to an afternoon at the Improv. As the nurse wheeled me out of the room to x-ray my ankle, Mark told her to examine my head while she was at it.

It all turned out okay. The hardware holding everything together was still intact, and Mark chained me to the couch after that, so I wouldn't kill myself. But I remained haunted by the memory of stinking in the spotlight.

I spent a good part of my life trying to cover myself and my tracks. The underlying fear was that someone might discover who I really was. Heck, *I* didn't even know who I was, but it couldn't be good. I was in my own Garden of Eden after the fall, furiously hunting in the woods for something big enough to cover myself with. Unfortunately, fig leaves don't come in size twelve.

Now if God had really been thinking ahead, He would have put 8 days in the week, and spent that last day creating a place where a girl can get some comfort food and decent coverings. "Let there be a large super-store, and let it provide pizza rolls and M&Ms and an abundant supply of women's clothing in sizes 4 – 22." And He called the super-store Walmart. And He saw that it was good.

You've probably heard this popular expression in Christian circles: "More of God, less of me." Some even take that a step further and say, "All of God, none of me." You know something? GOD LIKES YOU! He doesn't want to eliminate you. If anything, He wants more of you. Let it all hang out there.

I wonder if Adam and Eve had any complaints after God made them. Adam may have wished he wasn't so hairy, and Eve might have wanted smaller feet. But they didn't feel the need to cover themselves until after they listened to the wrong voice. Could that be the reason some people are getting nose jobs, hair plugs and liposuction? I'm just sayin' …

I guess there comes a time when we have to stop covering ourselves, afraid we'll be embarrassed by who we really are. Everything God made is good. He made the water and said, "It is good." He made the land and said, "It is good." He made man and said "Hmm, this is … not so good." Nah, just kidding. He knew what He was doing when He made us. I guess you could say He has a sense of humor.

Just as I am, without one plea
But that thy blood was shed for me.

Just as I am. Just as you are. It is good. And if all else fails, just remember this: You are what you think, not what you think you are.

25

I'M HERE NOW AND THAT'S ENOUGH

"But seek first his kingdom and his righteousness, and all these things will be given to you as well. Therefore do not worry about tomorrow, for tomorrow will worry about itself." (Matt 6: 33-34)

"I don't want to be somewhere else anymore. Not waiting for anything new to happen, not looking around the next corner or hill. I'm here now, and that's enough." (Anthony Hopkins, 'Shadowland')

There was a time when I was obsessed with the mailman. I would look out the window twenty times a day to see if his truck was down the block where he always parked it. Once the truck finally got there, my obsession went from looking out the window to watching the clock. I knew it would take approximately an hour and a half for him to get to my house. Sometimes I would get irked because it took longer, in which case the mailman would get a lecture about being punctual and not stopping to talk to every Tom, Dick and Harry along the way.

I don't know exactly what I expected to get in the mail. I guess I was so desperate for something, anything good to happen. So, I put my hope in the mailman to bring me glad tidings from Publishers Clearing House, or a letter from a publisher saying they wanted to publish my book.

Mark would tease me about my neurotic tendencies, but he got sucked into it too, at times. One spring day a few years ago, we were keeping a close watch on the mail because we were expecting our tax refund. We took turns watching for the little white truck, the clock, and anything else that moved. And then—glory! The mailman finally arrived. Mark waited a respectable amount of time to retrieve the mail so he wouldn't appear desperate to the mailman, and then he reached into the mailbox and found the big yellow envelope. He was beside himself with joy. He whooped so loud, the mailman looked back to see what was going on. He was caught in the act, red-handed.

The trouble with this sort of psychotic behavior is, we never appreciate the moment we're in; we're always looking for something better around the corner. Matthew 6:31 says, "So do not worry, saying, "What shall we eat?" or "What shall we drink?" or "What shall we wear?" or in my case "What shall I get in the mail?"

Matthew 6:33 started to haunt me. I read it over and over, trying to understand what it meant to trade my kingdom for God's, and how one would go about doing that. I embarked on this strange new journey by spending the first few hours of each day with God. I worshiped Him, sat quietly in His presence, or kept my nose in the Bible.

One day while I was in my room with God, out of the blue He said, "Here comes your chair." I didn't have a chair in my bedroom, so when I got tired of standing, I would sit on the floor which resulted in a backache. I asked Mark if we could get a chair for our bedroom, and he said absolutely not, our bedroom was too small for any extra furniture. You would think I had asked for breakfast in bed.

So right after God said, "Here comes your chair," I heard a commotion downstairs. I went down to see what was going on. It was Mark and one of our boys carrying a rocking chair into the house. God laid it on Mark's heart to buy me a chair.

I began to understand that seeking God's kingdom means I can stop trying to line up all my ducks in a row. God will do that for me, in His own way and time. How can I even appreciate the moment at hand when my thoughts are drifting off into the future? I'm finally in that sweet place where I can say, "I'm here now and that's enough." No, that's more than enough!

So, what do you say? Are you ready to trade your kingdom for His? It sure beats putting all your faith in the mailman, though I'm not completely ruling out Publishers Clearing House. I just got a letter from them the other day. Apparently, I'm in the final running!

26

THE PHARISEE'S CORNER

"And when ye pray, ye shall not be as hypocrites, that love to pray standing in synagogues and in corners of streets, to be seen of men; truly I say to you, they have received their meed. But when thou shalt pray, enter into thy bedchamber, and when the door is shut, pray thy Father in huddles, and thy Father that seeth in huddles, shall yield to thee." (Matt 6:5-6 Wycliffe NT)

"Ask not what your country can do for you—ask what you can do for your country." (John F. Kennedy)

I get a kick out of that … "pray thy Father in huddles." Football teams huddle, but I don't know how one would go about huddling all by themselves. That old time Bible talk is some pretty swanky stuff.

My son Aaron and I have a special language of our own. I don't know when this started, or why, but whenever we talk on the phone, we talk in Elmer Fudd voices.

"Hewwo Awon!" I'll say, in a cheerful voice.

"Hewwo Momma Dude!" He'll respond.

Neither one of us has the stamina to carry on the entire conversation like that. At some point we go back into regular voice mode. But it's fun while it lasts. I enjoy these childlike conversations.

Did you ever hear a child pray? Their prayers are usually pretty simple. When my kids were little, their prayers went something like this: "Dear God, please give me a new bike, and a new game for my computer. And please make Tommy stop hitting me." At this point I would admonish them to say a few things they were thankful for, and that usually resulted in thanksgiving for things like toys, cookies and rainbows.

I wanted so much more for my kids. I wanted them to grow up in their prayer life and pray about things like world peace and third world countries. I was sure that God was pacing the heavens, anxiously awaiting the day when these simple prayers would take flight and turn into epiphanies of glorious, flowery expressions that would delight His heart.

I remember sitting in a Bible study a few years ago, where we would go around the room taking turns praying aloud. I was so terrified about sharing my pitiful prayers, that I would find myself gripping my chair with sweaty palms until my knuckles turned white. My brain was grasping for an escape route. Quick! Think of an excuse to get out of here! "I think I left something on at home; the gas, the water, something …" What if my prayers didn't sound as good as the next guy's? My reputation as a Christian would be ruined.

And as hard as I tried after that pathetic performance to make my words flowery in an Elizabethan English sort of way, I just never got good at it. Fear of man seemed to be bigger than fear of God, and it always won in the end. I always found myself trying to put on a show just like the Pharisee on the street corner. Ugh! Why couldn't I just worry about what God thought of me, instead of worrying about everyone else?

And then God hit me over the head with a two by four … ouch! The same judgment I feared was inflicted on my prayers, I was judging my kids with. Their sweet, simple prayers weren't satisfactory to me, when in fact, they were the ones who had it right all along.

God doesn't want us to go into training in order to talk to Him, He wants us to be real in our prayers, and speak from our hearts. It's just a conversation, it's not rocket science. In the same way that we feel comfortable spending time with a friend, we can be comfortable with God and not feel pressured to put on a performance.

When my kids want to sit down and talk to me, I don't send subliminal messages that I want their conversation in a certain format or expect them to recite big fancy words. I just want to hear what's on their hearts.

In the process of growing up in Christianity, it's inevitable that the things we pray for will change. A child prays for things that will bring him comfort and happiness. The prayer of a child is all about *me*.

At some point our prayers need to go from desiring our own comfort, to the comfort of others. Our prayers are still about me, but we change our focus from "outside in" to "inside out." Now we ask God to change *me*.

Make *me* a peacemaker. Help *me* to forgive those who have hurt me. Kick *me* in the pants when I see someone in need and don't automatically rush to their aid. And as God answers our prayers and refines us, this *will* lead to world peace, one prayer at a time.

What saith thee? Wilt thou huddle thyself for world peace?

27

HIDE AND SEEK

"God is with you, in everything you do" (Gen 21:22)

"It is difficult to know why God reveals Himself to some and plays the game of hide and seek with others."
(Baba Ramdas)

When I read this scripture for the first time, I probably had that "burglar caught in the motion detector light" look. What? God is with me? If I squint one eye tight and focus, can I see Him? My mind started reeling, thinking about all the times I said or did things that God might not have approved of.

Back in the day, I was a smoker. Mark knew that when we started dating, but he just assumed that because he didn't like it, that I would quit. When that didn't work, he ran over my silver cigarette case with his car. Flattened it like a pancake. He handed it back to me, saying "Stuff your cigarettes in *this*."

I did quit for a while, but I took up the habit again after we got married, which forced me to become a closet smoker. Do people actually smoke in closets? Geez, all that second-hand smoke could kill you!

No, I would go outside on the porch and puff away. That way my clothes didn't reek of smoke. And that, along with guzzling Listerine after each cigarette helped me to keep my dirty little secret. But after a while the guilt started getting to me, so I would bring my Bible along to ease my conscience. Yes, I'm smoking behind my husband's back, but I'm reading the Bible, so … it's okay. So there.

I was fooling everyone except God. He was right there beside me. He knew every move I made. I'm a little uncomfortable about that. The thought of Him accompanying me to the bathroom is rather disconcerting. I once said to Him, "You wait here, I have to go to the bathroom." But He came in anyway. "I told you to wait outside!" I cried indignantly.

I knew a woman who ran a Christian website. One day she made the comment that God doesn't know our thoughts; that He's too much of a gentleman to pry into our consciousness. Wait … what? Psalm 139:1-4 says, " You have searched me, LORD, and you know me. You know when I sit and when I rise; you perceive my thoughts from afar. You discern my going out and my lying down; you are familiar with all my ways. Before a word is on my tongue you, LORD, know it completely."

When we ask Him into our hearts, He takes up residency and dwells with us. If we welcome His presence, that's good. But if we don't, then we have to ask ourselves what we're trying to hide. If we could just get past trying to keep things from God. We can't keep any secrets. He sees everything we do.

The question is, do we know what *He* is doing? In John 5:19 Jesus said He only does what He sees the Father doing. What if instead of trying to keep Jesus from seeing what *we're* doing, we started trying to see what *He's* doing? Hide and seek might be a fun game to play, but God wants us to stop hiding and start seeking.

In a real relationship everything is out in the open.

Can you imagine living your life for two? I'd be holding doors open for God, saying "After You." Or debating a restaurant menu— "Will it be steak or lobster?" He'd probably say, "Neither. On that last shopping trip, you parted with your cash like you were parting the Red Sea. I told you those WWJD bracelets would go out of style by the end of the year."

We're learning to get along, God and me. It's all good.

28

OPEN SEASON ON STUFFED ANIMALS

"The Lord is right in everything he does. He is loving toward everything He has made." (Ps 145:17 NIRV)

"It's knowing that I'm going to take life from something that treasures life as much as I treasure mine. It's the planning ahead, going looking for it, hunting for it that makes it murder. I'm right sick about it."
(John Boy Walton in *The Hunt*.)

You've heard the story before. A child begs his parents for a dog. They promise to take care of it. Guess who ended up taking care of the dog. Yep. Otis is downright adorable, but he has some undesirable flaws. When he drinks water from his dish most of it drips back out of his mouth all over the floor. Sometimes our floor looks more like a lake. And whenever I bring out the mop to soak up the water or the vacuum cleaner to clean up the dog hair, he runs. He probably gets that from me. I have the same reaction to cleaning supplies.

Otis is needy and demands attention constantly. First thing in the morning he's running after me the minute I get out of bed, for his daily dose of love. But if I haven't had my coffee yet, it's every man, woman and beast for themselves. I once heard a preacher say that God convicted him he needed to be nicer to his dog. I was stunned when I heard that! I thought we only had to be nice to people.

Last summer we were camping one night when the raccoons started coming around. We watched them fight over everything from leftover hot dogs to burnt marshmallows. When their claws come out it can get pretty ugly.

A guy who was camping down the road came over to our campsite to watch the show. He remarked that it would be funny to put something in the food that would make the raccoons sick. I didn't give that comment a second thought, but apparently God did.

That night I dreamt that our granddaughter was throwing up in front of our camper. I was deeply troubled, because in the dream I knew someone had poisoned her. Was God showing me that He feels equally distressed when someone tortures one of His animals? I recalled a recent visit to a nature center where I had sensed God's sorrow, but I didn't know why He was grieving. In light of this dream, I wondered if He was grieving for all the animals that had been sacrificed for the pelts and stuffed critters on display. I read in the newspaper about a couple who travels around the world to hunt down exotic animals, and then they subject them to taxidermy so they can display their trophies in their home. The animals are God's trophies, not ours.

In the book of Jonah, God said this about the animals: "And should I not have concern for the great city of Nineveh, in which there are more than a hundred and twenty thousand people who cannot tell their right hand from their left—and also many animals?" (Jonah 4:11). Here God's concern wasn't just for the people, but for the cattle on the hills.

Over and over in the Bible we read that God, out of His great compassion, spares people, which I get, but going out of His way for the animals brings compassion to a whole new level.

I was never an animal lover until I finally understood just how much God loves them. I even wondered why God went through all the trouble of loading all of the animals into the ark to save them from the flood, when   He could just as easily have wiped them out and whipped up a whole new batch after things settled down. Even Noah may have questioned God's love for the animals as he was cleaning up all the dung in the ark. "Lord, you're kidding, right? You can't seriously want to save a species that can't clean up after themselves!"

Why does God even care about something that doesn't have a soul? Probably because all of His creation carries His DNA. God loves everything He made; everything that He breathed life into. He said that we can eat the animals for food (Gen 9:3), but that certainly doesn't include hunting them down for sport (Proverbs 12:10), much less stuffing them. He wants us to enjoy His creation while it's still living, not after it's dead and stuffed. I don't think God likes stuffed animals. Now don't go all bona fide on me. Winnie the Pooh and Tickle Me Elmo are okay.

I have come to the conclusion that if God loves animals all that much, the least I can do is reach down and pet Otis first thing in the morning, with or without coffee. I'm not even worried about my morning breath. He's got me beat in that department.

I'm no animal, but I'm going to start empathizing with their plight as if I'm one of them. Isn't that what Jesus did for us? By the looks of my bathroom mirror, I'm not that far away.

THE GOOD THE BAD AND THE UGLY

"I no longer call you servants, because a servant does not know his master's business. Instead I have called you friends, for everything that I learned from my Father I have made known to you." (John 15:15)

"There is not in the world a kind of life more sweet and delightful than that of a continual conversation with God." (Brother Lawrence)

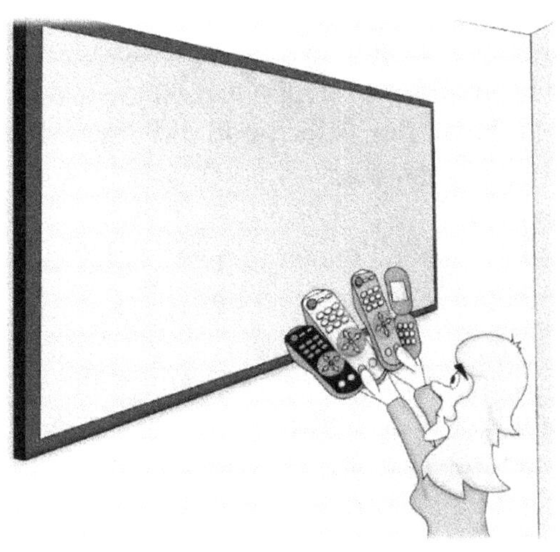

THE GOOD: Our kids chipped in and got us a big screen HD TV for Christmas, along with a Blu Ray player. I know, what? All this high-tech stuff. HD, R2D2, C3PO. It's all foreign to me. The picture on the tube is glorious, you should see the colors on this thing! It's so big and wild, makes me think I had some bad mushrooms.

THE BAD: I don't know how to work any of it. Let's start with the remote controls. There used to be one remote, and I aimed and fired that thing like there was no tomorrow. But now there's four of these bad boys! I'm picking them up one at a time, pressing all the buttons ... nothing. I'm holding all of them at once, clicking and aiming in every direction, slinging my weapons at every moving target. Nothing. Huh? One of these bad boys is ringing. Oh wait, looks like one of the remotes is actually the telephone. Okay, so we're down to three bad boys. I miss the good old days when I was smarter than my remote.

THE UGLY: I don't need to paint a picture for you, do I? Somebody's going to get hurt.

I'm so thankful God doesn't require us to learn how to use complicated equipment in order to talk to Him. If this twit had to tweet or text message a prayer, I wouldn't have a prayer! He made communication between heaven and earth a process that any simpleton could understand. It couldn't be any easier.

Recently a Christian blogger gave the opinion that if we want to talk to God, we must get on our knees. He said it's disrespectful to talk to God while we're sitting down or walking, or in any position other than kneeling. I'm all for the "knee" time, but if I could only talk to God while I was kneeling, some of our conversations would be limited to when I'm tying my shoes or smelling the carpet to see if it needs a good cleaning. The invitation God offers for intimacy doesn't make us His equals, but it does bestow the privilege of walking Hand in hand with our Creator. God is friend and Lord all at once, no matter our posture.

A servant might have to kneel before God in order to speak to Him, but God says we are no longer servants, but friends. I have a few friends (I know, can you believe it?), and I don't prostrate myself in order to have a conversation with them. We're a little more informal than that. We've been known to disagree with each other on occasion, and even to laugh at each other's foolishness.

I like to talk to God all day long, in many positions:

On my knees … I am GOOD. Good, repentant daughter. This is a good position to be in to humble myself before the Lord. When I'm on my knees I'm submitting to His Lordship and honoring His Majesty. He is King of Kings.

On my feet … I am BAD. Dangerous, even. Oh, the places I'll go! The stupid things I'll say.

When I'm on my feet, some of those dark thoughts that are racing around in my head are suddenly up and moving, with my feet as a vehicle. Like Paul, I do what I don't want to do, and I don't do what I should (Romans 7:15). That's why on my feet is the most important position to talk to God in. I am quick to call on Him to keep me out of trouble. If I have to wait until I can get on my knees, it may be too late.

Early in the morning … I am UGLY. I'm in no shape to face the world, but God welcomes me just as I am. He doesn't refuse my company until after I've brushed my hair and dropped to my knees. When I'm in that semi-conscious place between earth and La La land, snuggled in my blankets, it is there that God lavishes me in love. "On my bed I remember you; I think of you through the watches of the night" (Psalm 63:6). He must really love me, to hang in there even after He takes in my rooster hairdo.

Good … Bad … ugly … God wants it all!

THE BEST SEAT IN THE HOUSE

"These places belong to those for whom they have been prepared by my Father." (Matt 20:23)

"What lies behind you and what lies in front of you, pales in comparison to what lies inside of you."
(Ralph Waldo Emerson)

I like to have the best seat in the house when it comes to events like concerts and plays. And if I can't get there early enough to nab a good seat, I'll ask a friend to hold one for me. But getting a good seat in heaven is another matter entirely. It's not that I think I'm "all that," or that I want some recognition in heaven. No, I just want to be as close to Jesus as possible.

I wish I could just ask a saint who's on their way up to heaven to save a seat. I'd be like "Hey, Aunt Emma, if you get to heaven before I do, can you save a good seat for me?" But I'd have no way of checking on that. So, I took matters into my own hands and got busy with a game plan to get front row seats in heaven. I ushered at church, babysat in the nursery, and dutifully frowned upon the sinners smoking in the church parking lot.

In Rick Joyner's book, "The Call" Joyner talks about a series of dreams and visions he had in which he was taken up to heaven. When he got there, he was shocked to see many famous evangelists and preachers in the back of the room. He asked why they didn't end up closer to God's throne. They said it was because they had pride in their ministries.

Seated next to God was a man Joyner recognized as a homeless man he had seen on earth. He asked why this homeless man got to sit next to God. God said it was because the homeless man found a Bible, read it and treasured it, and made the cardboard box a temple of worship in which God was welcome to reside. The homeless man died one day in freezing temperatures while trying to keep another homeless man warm. I found it fascinating that the homeless man didn't travel around the world to work in mission fields or walk the streets preaching the gospel in order to get that coveted seat.

So just what did those people in the back of the room do that landed them there? I found a clue here: When Jesus sent out the seventy-two ahead of Him, they came back rejoicing that even the demons submitted to them, to which He replied, "Do not rejoice that the spirits submit to you but rejoice that your names are written in heaven" (Luke 10:20).

This is a very humbling statement. Rejoicing over casting out demons could result in pride—"Look at me, I'm casting out demons!" therefore they were advised to rejoice only in their salvation. "For it is by grace you have been saved, through faith—and this not from yourselves, it is the gift of God—not by works, so that no one can boast" (Eph 2:8-9).

There are a few examples in the Bible where people's works didn't get them very far. Take the prodigal son (Luke 15:11-32), for example. Here was a guy who just wanted to have a good time. He didn't want to run the farm or work the fields. And yet he was the guest of honor at the party; not his righteous, hard-working brother. And in the parable of the vineyard workers (Matthew 20:1-16), the field hands who came in at the last hour were paid just as much as the first truckload of guys who had been working all day. Where was the union when you needed it?

And then there's Mary and Martha (Luke 10:38-42). Martha was slaving in the kitchen while Mary rested at Jesus' feet, and Jesus said that Mary had it right. If only Martha had served the food buffet-style, or even ordered out for pizza, she could have saved herself a lot of work. The way to a *man's* heart is through his stomach, but not so with God.

Maybe God doesn't love the hard-working blue-or-white-collar guy any more than he does the down-on-his-luck sinner. I guess that would make Him "collar" blind. The slackers and sinners are the ones God is throwing a party for.

So, then I gave up trying to work my way to the front row, and went to the opposite extreme, saying "Could someone hand-feed me some grapes and wait on me hand and foot? I'm working on a plan for the best seat in the house!" But that attitude also works against the teachings of Jesus. "Anyone who wants to be first, must be the very last, and the servant of all" (Mark 9:35).

"Well, okay God," I said, "Then I'll just come right

out and ask for that seat!" But someone already beat me to it. James and John asked Jesus for good seats in heaven, to which He replied, "These places belong to those for whom they have been prepared by my Father" (Matt 20:23).

My wild goose chase for the best seat left me exhausted. I was just sitting here in my swivel chair at the computer, spinning around and around, when the thought came to me—"Where am I sitting right now? Am I close enough to God right here?" And I had to say … YES! And maybe that's all I need to worry about. How about you? Where's *your* best seat?

LIVING OUT LOUD

"Seize life! Eat bread with gusto, drink wine with a robust heart. Oh yes—God takes pleasure in your pleasure! Dress festively every morning. Don't skimp on colors and scarves. Each day is God's gift. Make the most of each one! Whatever turns up, grab it and do it. And heartily!" (Ecc 9:7-10 The Message)

"When you were born, you cried and the world rejoiced. Live your life in such a manner that when you die the world cries and you rejoice." (Indian saying)

I once drank so much coffee at a local coffee house that I got jittery to the point where I could have ground up my coffee beans with my hands. I even had difficulty driving the car after that caffeine overload. I could have been pulled over for speeding, and that was before I even took off! And when I made my way down the street, I had a heck of a time trying to remain calm so I wouldn't cause an accident. I was guilty of driving under the influence. How's that for gusto?

I was reading the story in 2 Kings 13:10-19, where Jehoash, king of Israel went to visit Elisha. Elisha instructed him to shoot an arrow out the east window, and then take the arrow and strike the ground with it. Jehoash struck the ground with the arrow three times which angered Elisha, who said that if he had struck the ground five or six times, he would have completely destroyed Aram, but now he would only defeat Aram three times.

Well, *that* makes sense … *non*sense! Nowhere does it say that Jehoash knew beforehand what striking the ground would signify? I hope Jehoash did his share of whining about the unfairness of that test. But somehow, I think this goes deeper. I'm picturing Jehoash as a shy, introverted kind of king. Maybe he had a history of shirking back instead of boldly forging ahead. Perhaps Elisha was projecting God's own displeasure with Jehoash. In the end, his apprehension cost him dearly.

Many people are shy and soft spoken, and there's nothing wrong with that. But there are probably many missed opportunities just like this one. If they had they only been a bit bolder and taken a chance, the journey would have been much more exciting and prosperous.

God created us to liven up this earthly kingdom, to dance with reckless abandon and dress festively every day. So why have we been trying to blend in with our drab outfits and personalities? We should make our marks and dress flamboyantly, like we're walking advertisements for a box of crayons.

Guys, how about rescuing that cartoon necktie from last year's Christmas present fiasco, and putting a smile on people's faces everywhere you go? Once you start living in color and boldly facing the road ahead, grabbing life with gusto should come fairly easy.

In the movie, "Yes Man" (which I am not recommending, due to some off-color scenes) Jim Carrey plays the part of Carl Allen, a man who has become withdrawn and preoccupied with his personal life after his wife divorces him. He spends all of his spare time in front of the TV and becomes a recluse. Then one day a friend invites him to a "Yes" seminar, where he is encouraged to seize the day and say "yes" to every opportunity that presents itself. By the end of the movie, he has learned how to play guitar, speak

Korean, fly an airplane, and much more. Now *this* is living!

See, the thing is, when I stand before God someday, I don't want to have any regrets about living a lackluster life. Do you? He went through all the trouble of creating each one of us unique and special. And now that we're all grown up, He's standing there with His hands on His hips looking us over, nodding His head in approval. "Oh yeah," He says, "I did good on this one!" Imagine His disappointment if we just turn into couch potatoes, wearing the same shirt we wore the last two days, and never venturing out into this great big world.

So, I'm challenging you to get up off the couch and make something happen. Write a poem, go skydiving, volunteer for the underprivileged, dance around the house in your underwear. Live man, live! Live each day like it's your last day here and beat that arrow into the ground like it's a metal detector hot on the trail of underground treasures. We're in the final frontier, so let's boldly go where no man has gone before. Yee haw!

About the Author

Debby is a wife, mother, grandmother, hippie at heart and friend of God. When she's not typing away at her keyboard like a mad scientist, she enjoys traveling, scrapbooking and sipping lemonade on her porch at the Hidden Valley Ranch.

Visit Debby at:

www.Facebook.com/InsideScoopOnGod

Debby has also co-written the award-winning *Mystery at Point Beach* series for teens with her partner in crime, Kate Jungwirth.

You can visit Kate and Debby at:

www.MysteryatPointBeach.com
www.Facebook.com/MysteryatPointBeach

Debby recently launched a sequel series to the *Mystery at Point Beach* books, called "The Tin Can Series." The first book in the series, *Mystery at Flaming Bay,* is available at Amazon.

If you enjoyed this book, would you consider posting a review on Amazon and Goodreads? We all need to laugh. It's good medicine.